Break Down the Walls

For he is our peace, who . . . has broken down the dividing wall of hostility. . . . And he came and preached peace to you who were far off and peace to those who were near (Ephesians 2:14, 17).

Break Down the Walls

A Christian Cry for Racial Justice

by

JOHANNES VERKUYL

edited and translated by

LEWIS B. SMEDES

WILLIAM B. EERDMANS PUBLISHING COMPANY
GRAND RAPIDS, MICHIGAN

Translated from the Dutch edition, *Breek de muren af! Om gerechtigheid in de rassenverhoudingen,* © 1971 Bosch & Keuning n.v., Baarn, The Netherlands.

To the memory of Zachariah Keodereleng Matthews, who, from his homeland in Fort Hare, South Africa, as servant of the universal church while in Geneva, and as ambassador to the United Nations from Botswana until the day of his death in May, 1968, gave his life to the ministry of reconciliation between the races of men.

Contents

Introduction

J. H. Oldham, who devoted his whole life to the struggle for justice between the races, died in 1969 at ninety-four in England. He wrote his germinal book, *Christianity and the Race Problem*, as far back as 1924. Oldham's notable service was to awaken us to the fact that the race question is not simply a matter of race, but a complex of economic, social, and political structures that have poisoned the relationship between races. He wrote his book at a time when the whole question of race relationships was being shaped and defined by the tensions between Western imperialism and colonialism on the one hand and the pressure toward national self-expression among the peoples of Asia and Africa on the other. The political-economic domination by white men during the period of colonialism and imperialism had twisted and distorted these relationships ever since the 16th and 17th centuries. Since Columbus discovered America and the conquistadores set out in quest of booty in South America, since Vasco da Gama sailed around Africa to India and Abel Tasman landed in Australia, the white race had gradually taken over seven-eighths of the globe. From 1500 until 1900 the white tidal wave had swept from the West to the South and the East. In this wave, the blessing of communication led to the curse of domination and servitude, colonialism and imperialism. Slowly but surely, however, the tide began to reverse. The reverse movement began at the end of the 19th and the beginning of the 20th century. The tide turned under the irresistible pressure for national self-expression, and with help from those powers in the West that were sympathetic toward this pressure, the decolonization process began and colonialism and imperialism in their familiar forms started their irrevocable decline.

Many people hoped that, with this, the racial question would solve itself. Their hope turned out to be a delusion. The emancipation of many people who had been ruled as colonies or who existed in semi-colonial status (as the people in Latin America) is still being fought for. Even the liberation movement among the Afro-American minorities, turbulently groping for full emancipation, is still in process.

The race question is no longer dominated by the tensions between colonialism and national self-identity. Now we have tensions between rich and poor lands and between poor minorities and affluent majorities (as the case may be) in white-dominated countries like the United States, Rhodesia, and South Africa. There is an unmistakable racial element in these tensions. The rich, highly industrialized lands (including Russia) have a generally white population, while the so-called "developing" lands are predominately nonwhite.

The question of world peace, of the survival of millions, even of humanity as a whole, depends in large part in the 20th century on a peaceful and just solution of the race question. Let me quote from U Thant, former Secretary General of the United Nations:

> It is clear that the growing racial conflict, if we do not succeed in controlling and eliminating it, is going to grow into a consuming monster, compared to which all the religious and ideological conflicts of the past will look like family squabbles. Such a conflict will destroy all possibilities for progress among the people of the world and will reduce mankind to the lowest and most bestial level of intolerance and hatred. For the sake of our children, regard-

less of their color, we must work with all the powers that are within us to prevent this from happening.

Lord Caradon and the black American novelist James Baldwin spoke in the same spirit at Uppsala, Sweden, on July 7, 1968, in an unforgettable evening in the aula of the university. They did not fantasize. Lord Caradon learned to know colored people through a lifetime devoted to the liquidation of colonialism. James Baldwin is a sensitive seismograph who translates with finely honed instrumentation the things that are stirring in the souls of black men in America and around the world.

Listen also to the voice of a woman. On March 16, 1969, Coretta King, the widow of Martin Luther King, Jr., preached a sermon from the pulpit of St. Paul's Cathedral in London, the first woman ever to have sermonized there in a regular worship service. Let me pass on a few words from her sermon:

> Throughout the world, we face the dangerous situation in which the largest share of the world's riches lies in the hands of that small percentage of the world's population which happens to be white, while the majority of the colored peoples is very poor. This is indeed an explosive situation. For they have heard the message that they are God's children. They have heard this message from the servants of the church as well as from the apostles of technology. This situation is complicated by the fact that the war machines of the great, technological Western blocs stand prepared to protect the privileges of those who already have more than their share of the material resources of the world.
>
> If we do not take care, our world will split along the line that divides whites from coloreds, rich from poor, the so-called developing countries and their millions from the technologically developed lands of the North. This is the time to proclaim the ministry of reconciliation. This is the time to proclaim the acceptable year of the Lord.

The present little book, then, is an effort to contribute to this ministry for the reconciliation of the races to which Mrs. King called us from the pulpit of St. Paul's Cathedral. It is written in the conviction that Jesus Christ is Lord of both the church and the world, and that He came to reconcile men, races, and nations with God and with one another. Somewhere in the Bible (we will come back to it) we are told that by His cross and resurrection He broke down the walls that separated peoples and races, and that He is bent on creating a new humanity, a genuinely new mankind, one man formed out of the many peoples and races. If true, this is not only the message of joy-producing promises and hope-inspiring acts, but a demand for us to translate the message into action. If it is really true that He has come to reconcile us with God and with one another, then the summons compels us: Reconcile yourselves with God and with one another. *If it is true that He has broken down the walls between men, then we are conscripted to join the work of demolition.* We must break them down instead of conspiring to buttress them—break down the walls of racial prejudice and racial discrimination, break down the structures in which racial pride and greed are invested, break down the social and economic walls that separate the poor and rich peoples of the world. Christians have no alternative. They must join the struggle against racial injustice and for racial justice.

James Baldwin said in Uppsala: "Most people are not scoundrels. But they are so frightfully lazy, and they are so terribly afraid to do anything." Yes, the rich lands are afflicted with the curse of inertia, a wretched lust for the pleasant life. It comes down to us, whether we can be counted on to participate in the struggle—to break down the walls!

We must believe that it is *possible* for a generation to arise in the face of struggle and actually break down walls and transform the structures. When the time came in the 18th and 19th centuries to stop the slave trade and put an end to slavery, there was incredible resistance, the resistance of laziness and inertia, resistance from vested interests and from structures of violence. But the humanists and the Christians kept at the struggle, spurning the temptations to compromise. And they prevailed. Now that the time has come to support the liberation of the colored peoples of the world, we must not drag our feet, must not give up, must not betray Christ. Now is the time to push the issue through to victory.

Along with all there is to be ashamed of in our time, there is still reason for hope. The younger people of all racial groups are today demonstrating more understanding of each other and greater sensitivity to racial injustice than has ever been experienced in our time. It is the attitude of the younger generation that has pushed me into writing this book.

Finally, a word about the perspective from which I will be looking at the entire racial question. We could select any one of many standpoints from which to analyze the question. We could look at it from the viewpoint of biology, or anthropology, or sociology. Or, we could set it within the perspective of the history of culture, of linguistics, or, of course, of political science or economics. A steady stream of books written on the race question from these various points of view has added a great deal to my own enrichment. But I do not wish to repeat the material taken from these studies, not even to summarize them. I am writing out of a desire to reach out for God's promises and to obey His demands for relationships among the races. Human actions must, in this area as in others, be guided by God's promises and God's commands. In the racial question, too, we are involved with conversion and obedience. The decisive question is never, What says my blood, my group, my people, my Western culture? The deep and decisive question is, What does the Lord want us to do?

This book seeks an answer to this question, and we want to seek it in fellowship with everyone who seriously asks the question for himself.

Chapter One

The Concept of Race

WHAT RACE IS NOT

We must begin with the elementary question, What do we mean by the words "race" and "races"? The theologians cannot give us an answer to this question. We must ask the experts, the cultural anthropologists and the like. The most illustrious among them, people like Frans Boaz, Melville Herklovitch, Margaret Mead, Ruth Benedict, Eugene Nida, and the authors of the UNESCO studies on race, usually begin by telling us what a race is not. This is a good thing to do, because popular notions about race are profoundly confused.

For instance, race is frequently identified with language: We speak of the Aryan languages as the languages of the Aryan race, of Chinese as the language of the Chinese race, English as the language of the English race. But language has little to do with race. English is spoken by millions who belong to an entirely different race than the original ethnic groups found in England. This holds true of French, Turkish, and Chinese as well. Race is a biological concept. Language is a cultural concept.

We should not confuse race and culture either. No proof has ever been given that the color of skin or hair, the shape of the nose, the form of the head, or whatever other biological variations, have anything to do with mental or cultural differences. Racial differences bear little relation to the development of cultures, at least compared to the milieu in which particular groups live and to the historical forces that influence their development. Environment and locale define cultures; races do not. Culture is not a racial function. Every study that has set out to show a correlation between race and culture has reached dead end. Culture, Ruth Benedict remarks flatly but with undeniable accuracy, is not the shibboleth for differences in race. In April of 1965, the UNESCO *Courier*, a publication by biological and cultural anthropologists, underscored this anew.

Cultures have been interracial in their genesis and development, and we all participate more and more in a world culture to which all peoples have contributed and which is being adopted everywhere. The progress that has been made for the last thousand years has been due in increasing measure, if not exclusively, to culture and the transfer of cultural achievements rather than to the transmission of biological and genetic inheritances. The use of steel was developed in India, and all peoples have taken its use into their cultures. The American Indians taught the world to use corn and tobacco. The Arabs taught us algebra. The people of Northern India taught us how to use the number zero. The Chinese introduced us to the uses of herbs, and they discovered typography. We learned how to use the calendar from the Babylonians, irrigation from the Incas, and terracing from the Indonesians. Even modern science and technology is an international, not an exclusively Western, contribution. The concept "racial culture," then, makes no sense.

That religious beliefs and practices are not segregated racially is so apparent that it hardly needs mentioning. Yet, Christendom is commonly identified with the so-called "Western race," and the Moslem and Buddhist religions with other races, though a child can see that the religions of the world are not parceled out according to race.

Nor are racial distinctions a national matter. It was never so in the past, and certainly is not today. North Americans do not constitute a race; they are a huge constellation of races. But the same holds for the English, the French, the Lebanese, the Nigerians, the Latin Americans, and all the others. No single modern nation contains people of a single race. Every nation is interracial even though in many instances one race may be predominant.

WHAT RACE IS

We are concerned here with the concept of race as it is used in modern scientific senses. The word "race" is not very old. Some think it comes from the Italian word *razza,* which means "line," as in bloodline or genealogical line. Others see it as coming from the Arabic word *ra's,* which means "origin." But we are not as concerned with the etymology of the word as with the concept of race used by modern science, and that is roughly equivalent to such phrases as "ethnic groups" or "series of ethnic groups."

Sometimes in reaction to the many false notions of what a race is people conclude that the notion of race must be fictional, that no such thing as a race actually exists. But this is not realistic. The concept of race does point to a reality. It is a *biological* concept. There are obvious biological variations in the human family, and we can point to characteristics that distinguish one race from another.

Around 1948, UNESCO set a large number of experts to work on the historical, biological, psychological, and sociological aspects of racial variations. The results of their work were published in a series of brief studies under the umbrella title of *The Race Question in Modern Science.* Then in 1952 a single booklet, *The Race Concept, The Results of an Inquiry,* brought together the several studies. I have borrowed the following conclusions from this booklet.

(1) Scholars have reached a consensus that humanity is one, that all men belong to the same species called Homo sapiens. Further, the consensus is that all men probably have a common origin, and that the differences among various groups of the human race came about as a result of evolutionary factors, factors such as isolation, the movement and accidental fixing of the material particles which control inheritance (genes), changes in the structure of these genes, crossing, and natural selection. In this way, racial groups arose out of variations in stability and variations in the degree of differentiation.

(2) Seen from a biological standpoint, the human species consists of a number of racial or ethnic groups that differ from one another according to the presence or absence of certain genes. Such genes, which cause inherited differences among people, are always limited in number compared with the total genetic constitution of man and in comparison with the large number of genes that people possess in common, irrespective of the ethnic group to which they belong. This means that what men have in common is far greater than their differences.

(3) Racial groups form, as it were, variations on the theme of man. In short, the term "race" loosely indicates a group of people among whom certain characteristics appear that are caused by concentrations of inherited particles (genes), characteristics that surface, fluctuate, and often disappear again in the course of time as a result of geographic or cultural isolation.

In 1965, UNESCO issued a new publication supporting these conclusions and working them out in greater detail. I don't think it necessary within the limits of this study to expand on the details. But I would like to mention a few physical characteristics of race.

The most obvious difference is in the color of skin. But while skin color may be most often used to distinguish between races, it is in fact the least useful. Some Caucasian groups in India are darker than Negroids, though Caucasians are popularly classed as white and Negroids as black. There are groups of people in North Africa whose skin is much the same as the Negroids, and yet they are Europeans. And we could go on.

More reliable indicators are the color and shape of the eyes, the color and texture of the hair, the shape of the nose (narrow or broad), and the types of various blood groups. Some time ago, the shape and weight of the brain were thought to play a large role in distinguishing between races. But it slowly became evident that significant differences in the shape and weight of the brain were common *within* racial groups, and this factor fell away as a means of distinguishing between races. The other characteristics have more or less survived through inheritance and in the course of centuries have become indicators of certain races or subgroups within races.

RACIAL CATEGORIES

Anthropologists draw up a variety of categories. Their methods for classifying are not uniform. But there is pretty large agreement as to main groups. The three main classes are Caucasoids, Mongoloids, and Negroids. Frans Boaz, one of the best-known experts in this field, says that there are really only two main groups—the Mongoloids and the Negroids—and that Europeans actually belong to the Mongoloids. But, as a general rule, the three main classes are kept distinct.

These three are then usually subdivided:

Caucasoids: the people of North India, the North Europeans, the Alpine people (Central Europeans), and the Mediterranean peoples.

Mongoloids: the Mongolian people (the Chinese, the Vietnamese, the Thais, the Tibetans, etc.), the Malaysian people (Malaya and the majority of the Indonesian population), and the American Indians.

Negroids: the Negroes, the Melanesians, the Negritos, and the indigenous tribes of South Africa.

Somewhere outside of these three main groups fall the following: the Australoids (the so-called aborigines of Australia), the Polynesians, the Veddoids (of Ceylon), and a people of North Japan known as the Ainus.

Variations and mixtures among all the groups are legion. The notion of a "pure race" is sheer fiction, created by demagogues and "professors" who deal in pseudo-ideologies and other forms of superstitions. Melville J. Herklovitch, one of the most respected anthropologists of our time, points out that even in a biological sense the most homogeneous groups consist of mixtures, that in deed in the course of their histories racial groups undergo a long series of mixtures.

From earliest times, an incredible amount of mixing has taken place through the migrations of people over the earth. Cultural anthropologists tell us that in their field of research there is no more remarkable phenomenon than the way people, often against enormous obstacles, have spread out over the earth and have mixed among other peoples. Civilizations have arisen everywhere in the world out of these mixtures of races. We need only mention the Greek, the Roman, the Chinese, and the Mesopotamian cultures to give a hint of how this has happened.

Chapter Two

The Biblical Message
and the Race Question

IS THERE A MESSAGE?

The concept of race, in the strict modern sense, is a
fairly recent one. In the modern sense, the idea of race is
not even found in the Bible. Racial consciousness, racial
antagonism, racial conflicts are phenomena we meet in
the framework of the social, political, and economic
structures of recent world history. They just do not, in
that sense, enter the horizon of the people who wrote the
Bible.

Without denying this, we must contend that the biblical light of God's promises and demands profoundly
illuminates our struggles with these modern problems. At
the deeper level of everything that touches on the race
question—discrimination, injustice, and power blocs of
racial groups (white, black, brown, red)—lies the question, What do you think of man, and what do you expect
of him? What motives, what norms, what ends define
your attitudes and behavior toward racial groups other
than your own? Where and how do you go about looking
for answers to these questions?

The path through the many questions about race runs
along a mountain way with deep ravines on either side.
We could slip on both sides of the path. We really do

need the light of God's promises and demands to keep
from falling. This is why we want to begin by opening the
Bible and asking God for His light.

An analysis of the Bible's message concerning the relationships between people and groups will not be enough.
We surely have to do more than to repeat some texts. We
shall have to follow up our biblical discussion with talk
about today's specific situations and societies. But when
we get to the concrete challenges of our day, we must try
not to forget what we learned from the Bible. If we do
get some light from God, we would be stupid not to use
it to help us see where we have got to walk here and now
in believing obedience to God's promises and demands. It
seems to me that a lot of the literature on the race
question ignores the relevance and significance of the
Bible—the problems and responsibilities involved in it are
too often lost. So I suggest we dig somewhat more
seriously than most writers on the subject into the biblical word for race relations.

THE FUNDAMENTAL UNITY
OF THE HUMAN FAMILY

We may begin with the observation that the Bible, as
profoundly as it does simply, as divinely as it does hu-
manly, reveals that the human family is in principle one.
Genesis 1 and 2 gives us the story of the beginning of the
human race, the story of *ha-Adam—the* man. We can
appreciate how remarkable this story is only as we set it
alongside the racial or tribal myths of the ancient peoples, or, for that matter, of the Germans, the Japanese,
the Toradiahs and the Ibos, the Greeks and the Indians.
In the racial myths we always have a story of the original
ancestors of a certain *tribe* or *nation*. The people of other
tribes are only, as the Greeks put it, barbarians—people
who speak an absurd language—or devils, as in the old
Chinese myths, or other lesser beings.

The Genesis story is wholly unique in the entire world

of literature of this kind. It is not a tribal or national myth. It does not glorify one tribe of men over the others. Adam means *man*. The word Adam is not used in Genesis 1 and 2 as a personal name, but as a species name: *ha-Adam,* the man, that which has been made human, manhood. Genesis 1 and 2 tells us about man and humanity, not about a superhuman ancestor of a superior tribe of men.

Genesis 1 and 2 is put to hard questions these days, questions that touch on what its message really is. Naturally, the passage was never intended to provide lessons in biology, a descriptive account of a development of living beings, or to tell us exactly what we must think about anthropogenesis. It cannot even decide for us whether man came from a single or from several lines of origin. But its intention is clearly to bring us God's own word, never to be forgotten, and always to be used as our point of departure for how we think about one another and how we relate to one another.

The message has several parts. One of them is that all people on earth, from whatever race, are members of a single human family and form a unity. Amid all the arguments that have zeroed in on Genesis 1 and 2, this basic message is often strangely missed. When it comes to Genesis, we are often like David who heard Nathan's word about the lamb, but could not grasp what the prophet was trying to tell him about *himself.* Until the lightning fell, the word came: *You* are the man. There are thousands of Bible-believers who want to keep faith with the message of Genesis and still cannot hear God's judgment in it, a judgment on every political theory and every social and economic practice that does not root itself in *the unity of the human family*.

I once heard a black man relate what the message meant to him. He said: "For me, this message has taken all the nonsense-notions of races and turned them on their heads." He heard it right. When Paul stood before the Greeks on the Areopagus, he proclaimed the biblical message in these words: "God has made from one every nation of men to live on all the face of the earth" (Acts 17:26). *The unity of the human species is the point of departure for everything the Scriptures tell us about man.* And the same unity has been supported increasingly by scientific research.

In the first place, it has been supported by physiological anthropologists, people whose business it is to study human beings in their physiological aspects. Men everywhere are characterized by a vertical walk, by the same skull shape, the same general brain weight, the same general number of ribs, the same general pulse-beat, the same potential for mixing, the same length of pregnancy, and so on and on. All these features convince the physiological and biological anthropologists of the unity of the phenomenon of man.

The unity is much more impressive than are the variations. If one asks how the variations arose, the experts point to the influence of milieu, climate, diet, isolation, and the like. They talk about particular chemicals that all people carry inside themselves. These chemicals (especially carotene and melanin), under the influence of the sun's heat, cause variations in the color of the skin. Further, they indicate the influence of inheritance on the development of variations. But, however accounted for, the variations are never as impressive as the sameness and can never lead anyone to doubt the unity of the species.

The anthropologists who concern themselves with the psychic side of man also assume the unity of the human race. Everywhere among men we find the phenomena of language, logic, moral consciousness, religiosity, social and economic insight, aesthetic awareness—in short, a tendency toward cultural self-expression. This fact increasingly compels the social and psychic anthropologists to assume the fundamental unity of the human family.

But what may be a working hypothesis for the sciences is a firm conviction of Christian faith: Humanity is a unity.

Herman Bavinck had his finger on the crucial importance of human oneness. "It is the foundation of religion and morality. The solidarity of the human family, redemption in Christ, the universality of the Kingdom of God, the catholicity of the church, the law of love—these are all rooted in the unity of mankind." It is also decisive for the race question. The unity of mankind must be the point of departure, both for theory and practice, for anyone who concerns himself with the race question.

Never has the point been so much in need of making. The unity of the human family has never been as open to experience as it is now. Time was when various races had practically no contact with one another. Many racial groups existed in virtual isolation. But the very possibility of isolation is gone forever. We stand at the threshold of a period in which communication between racial groups is going to take place in a way that other generations never dreamed of. This is the era in which everything is going to depend on whether we are prepared to obey, at the experiential level, the message the Bible proclaims about the unity of our race.

THE DIVERSITY OF THE PEOPLES

The same Bible that declares the unity of the human race tells us that a great diversity has grown out of the unity. The Bible puts this diversity in a very different context than, say, sexual differences or age differences. The sexual distinction is obvious, of course. Men and women are both human, both created in God's image, both of equal value for God. But there is a male way to be human and there is a female way to be human, and the difference enriches life beautifully. But the Bible looks at the cultural differentiation of man differently than it does the sexual. How so? The sexual differentiation is a given, along with creation, of human existence. God intended human beings to live as male and female from the beginning. But the racial or ethnic variations are not an ordinance of God. They arose in the course of history.

The Bible merely observes this fluidity, and does it with
gratified surprise.

The differentiations appear explicitly in the well-
known "table of nations" found in Genesis 10. Here we
find the progenies of Noah, Shem, Ham, and Japheth.
Earlier chapters give a hint of the various groups, but
they do not make them explicit. In those chapters all the
stress is put on the unity of the race. But in Genesis 10
we feel a sense of surprise as the writer tells us how the
descendants of Noah, carried along by God's promises
and surrounded by His faithfulness, attested in the rain-
bow, have come to be so varied in their later development. All those branches flourish out of the root of a
single human being and are destined for reunification.

Gerhard von Rad has a fine discussion in his *Theology
of the Old Testament* of this so-called "table of nations."
He points out that Genesis 10 forms the climax of the
creation story. It underscores once more the unity and
universality of the human family, but now lets us see the
fulness of variety in which the substance of unity expresses itself.

If Genesis 10 had the structure of a myth, one people—
in this instance, Israel—would be set in the center, and all
the other peoples would figure as bit-players and satellites
revolving around the main group in centerstage. In Genesis 10, however, Israel does not appear at all. The universality of the peoples of the world is expressed in the
thought that all generations stem from the sons of Noah.
"With this the creaturely unity of humanity is expressed
with a clarity that knows no equal in the entire ancient
world." Von Rad goes on to point out that the register is
entirely free from race in its listings: it is wholly carto-
graphic, after the style of the times in which the table
was made, reflecting the political-historical divisions in
the second millennium before Christ.

No particular people gets top billing. They all appear
without distinction before God's face. God plans to be
occupied with them all in His great drama of redemption.

Karl Barth, in his *Church Dogmatics*, stresses the point that Genesis 10 does not present the variations as a kind of ordinance. The notion that the variations of peoples and ethnic groups present us with a divinely willed and divinely sustained "ordo creationis" Barth brands as pure whim, and says that to anyone who listens carefully to God's will and message the very thought is laughable. Genesis 10 reports the variations in the peoples of the world simply as a fact. It is not presented as something decisive, constant, permanent, or absolute. Precisely in the light of Genesis 10, every dogma of divinely willed racial differences is a heresy, every service given to the god of racial ideology is service rendered to a false god, an offering made on strange altars.

This episode in the biblical message does not oblige us to study the relationship between the peoples listed in the "table of nations" and the peoples familiar to us in our time. These stories simply make use of the knowledge that the writers had of the population of their day. They are not meant to be an atlas of the world's population in any scientific sense. The "table of nations" is meant to move us to grateful awareness of how the one human family manifests itself in countless, changing variations. The same note is sounded in other parts of the Bible. The New Testament uses all sorts of ways to express this diversity. I shall mention only one example.

The word *ethnos* (people), which forms the basis for the term "ethnology," points to the peoples in their biological diversity and in their variety of customs. (*Ethnos* is closely associated with *ethos*.) The word *laos* points more directly toward variations in political and social organization. The word *phulē* suggests the smaller ethnic unities within a people, and generally means the same as what we call a clan or tribe. The word *glossē* (language) indicates the unity that language provides for a given group.

These words are repeated frequently in the New Testament. (Hebrew equivalents for them appear in the Old

Testament.) They all appear together in Revelation 5:9 ff. There, the variety of tribes, peoples, and languages is not considered an impoverishment, but an enhancement of humanity. The creature man expresses himself in countless ways. God never wished for mankind to be a monotonous grey wall but a rich mosaic. God wants us human beings to complement one another, to complete each other, and with that to serve and support one another.

What sorts of diversity do we have in mind? To classify the patterns of variation is impossible. Every human formula is trite, too quickly given, and ends up as an irresponsible generalization. Why?

In the first place, it is questionable whether our so-called "folk-traits" or "racial attributes" are really genealogical types or whether they are phenomenological types. Do they arise from some enduring biological or psychological structure of a people or race, or are they the effects of climate, a milieu, history, culture, or social circumstances? No one can tell for sure. But what is certain is that the latter factors are more important than the first.

In the second place, it is not possible to classify the diversities of men because there are many variations within racial groups. Eugene Nida offers an interesting example of this in his book *Customs and Cultures*. It is often said of the African black men that they are very extroverted, talkative, warm, friendly. But there are also Negroid peoples who are very introverted, quiet, worrisome, and distrustful. I myself recall a Western teacher instructing an Eastern student on the distinctions between Eastern and Western mentalities. You will recognize the clichés. Emotional (East) and rational (West); passive (East) and active (West); contemplative (East) and volitional (West); spiritual (East) and materialistic (West); monistic (East) and dualistic (West); synthetic (East) and analytic (West). And so forth. After the lecture was finished, the student from the East said: "Professor, I have sat here at this conference for a whole week, listening to your characterizations. I must honestly say that I felt that your Western mentality fit me and your Eastern mentality fit you." The student was probably right. At any rate, he was on target to the extent that our efforts to classify the diverse characteristics of mankind are for the most part unfounded generalizations that scarcely touch down on reality.

In the third place, it is dangerous to classify the diversity because human pride tends to use classifications to demonstrate the superiority of one race over others. Every group, every people, every "race" has an inner urging to consider itself superior and to consider the other group or "race" inferior. Every group has a collective urge to self-deification; the Bible teaches us this and so does experience. Collective sin comes more clearly to light in collective judgments of the "other races" than anywhere else. Evidence that most people have this compulsion can be gathered at almost any cocktail party or kaffee-klatsch when no members of the "other group" are present. For these three reasons, in my judgment, it is impossible to classify the variations between peoples and races, and dangerous to try.

But this does not mean that there are no diversities. Mankind is not uniform; thank God it is diverse. We ought to acknowledge the pluriformity, and gratefully accept it.

Within the family of races, no one of them can say to another: I have no need of you. As the human body consists of many members, so does the body of mankind. God intends that the millions of people on the earth should learn to love one another, serve and help one another to become authentic human beings within one all-embracing fellowship. This variety does not even begin to diminish the unity of mankind. The racial differences are relative, very changeable, and have nothing at all to do with a creation ordinance.

In this survey of the biblical vision of the variations

within the peoples of the world, we have taken no notice of the remarkable passage of Genesis 9:24-27, which, in the course of the centuries, has been shamefully misused to deny the unity and equality of all men before God. By way of a brief excursion, let us talk about this passage.

THE HAM NONSENSE

The well-known story of Noah's blessing on Shem and Japheth and his curse on *Canaan* has been scandalously manipulated through several centuries to defend slavery and bring incalculable injury to Negroid peoples. My own anger at the way that this passage has been abused is so intense that I was inclined not even to mention it. But as the meaning of Genesis 1-11 began to excite me anew, I determined to take a new look at this passage. Dr. H. Leene, of the Free University of Amsterdam, was kind enough to be my guide through some recent commentaries on the passage and to provide me with a few notes from which I shall draw for the comments that I offer here—with his kind consent. Before going on to the commentary, however, we should notice some of the manipulations this passage of Scripture has suffered in the past.

A. Pseudo-Theological Manipulations of Genesis 9:24-27

It is no secret that Bible texts can be manipulated. In the story of Jesus' temptations in the wilderness (Matt. 4) even Satan manipulates Old Testament texts. But churches and theologians, too, are not immune to the temptation to manipulate biblical texts so as to build pseudo-biblical defenses behind which they can defend themselves against the promises and demands of God. One of the worst examples is the pseudo-theology built out of this passage.

The 18th century was the century both of the slave trade and of the subjection of Eastern and Southern peoples, along with the drive to exploit the Western hemisphere. Naturally, the whole movement was pestered by a bothersome thing called the Christian conscience. What response was made to murmurings of the conscience? On the one hand, men tried to defend themselves against conscience with the use of texts from the Bible. On the other hand, we find hints that men were sufficiently convicted by the message of the Bible to protest against the pseudo-theology that distorted it.

In the 18th and 19th centuries, there appeared in both England and America, as well as in the Netherlands and South Africa, a good many theological writings that used Genesis 9 to defend slavery and the slave trade, and to whitewash other forms of servitude. The Negroid peoples were established as the descendants of Ham—that is, burdened with a crippling inherited handicap and ordained by God to a status of subjection. The worst specimen of this literature is the infamous essay by Joseph Priest, *A Bible Defense of Slavery*. The whole book rests on the nonsense of Ham-theology.

The number of English, American, and Continental writers who figured in this theological prostitution is legion. But a particularly striking and sad instance in my own country of the Netherlands was Jacob Elisa Johannes Capitein, the first black preacher, who studied at the University of Leiden in the 18th century. This early black preacher himself defended slavery and recommended its re-institution in the Netherlands in the case of loafers. He made his case in an academic oration, given in Latin on March 10, 1742, under the chairmanship of his Leiden professor, J. van den Honert. Its title was *Dissertatio politico-theologica de servitude libertati christianae non contraria*, or *Political-Theological Dissertation Concerning Slavery As Being Consistent With Christian Liberty*. The Dutch translation saw four printings. The foundation of the argument was the old Ham-theology. The status of subjection to which the sons of Ham were doomed was not, the thesis went, in conflict with the Gospel. Evangelical freedom was spiritual and could be enjoyed under the condition of slavery as well as under any other physical condition. Those who attacked slavery on the basis of the Gospel manifested the "affections and manners of fanatics." Naturally, the operators of the Compagni were enormously gratified by this apology for slavery from a liberated black man. The oration was not only translated and reprinted, but celebrated in several poems. A. Eekhof, who in 1917 extensively studied this incident in the Netherlands Archive for Church History, tells us that there is no hint that anyone objected at the time to this extraordinary defense of Ham-theology.

Yet, there were some protests in the 18th century against the manipulation of Genesis 9. Several men who in the name of Christ and conscience attacked the pseudo-theological defenses of slavery are worth mentioning. Judge Samuel Sewall of Boston wrote *The Selling of Joseph* in 1700. The two Quakers John Woolman and Benjamin Franklin, the Methodist revivalist John Wesley, the Huguenot Anthony Benezet, and many others contributed to the protest in America. The manipulation of the Genesis passage has endured longest in South Africa. But even there, men like Ben Marais and S. du Toit have so thoroughly discredited this pseudo-theology that it is slowly but surely losing its grip.

B. *Notes Toward an Interpretation of Genesis 9:24-27*

> When Noah awoke from his wine and knew what his youngest son had done to him, he said, "Cursed be Canaan; a slave of slaves shall he be to his brothers." He also said, "Blessed be Shem; and let Canaan be his slave. God enlarge Japheth, and let him dwell in the tents of Shem; and let Canaan be his slave." (Gen. 9:24-27)

> The book of the genealogy of Jesus Christ, the son of David, the son of Abraham. (Matt. 1:1)

> And Judah the father of Perez and Zerah by Tamar.... (Matt. 1:3)

> And Salmon the father of Boaz by Rahab.... (Matt. 1:5)

What function does this passage in Genesis 9 perform within the whole of the Genesis story? It forms a prelude to the promises God gave to Abraham that his descendants would inherit the land of Canaan. The promise elicits from the reader an obvious question: "Why should the Canaanites be pushed out of their land?" Does the fate of the Canaanites not make nonsense of the promise that "In you all the families of the earth shall *be blessed*" (Gen. 12:3)?

The writer's point is, in fact, to answer this question. Canaan was being punished for his sins. He behaved in the same way that Ham did toward Noah. In Noah's blessing, the promise would come true through *Japheth*: All families of the earth were to be blessed. But Canaan is the exception for the time being, an exception that would last until the Canaanites too bowed their heads under Jahweh's hands of blessing.

The Jewish commentator Cassuto points out that in the Noah story Canaan represents the Canaanites who were Israel's neighbors in Palestine. The Israelites, Japhites, and Canaanites all confronted one another in a precarious balance of power in Palestine. We must read Genesis 9:24-27 from the point of view of a person living in *that* tense situation. We have got to read the very emphatic clause, "Ham is the father of Canaan" as though it is saying this: "Consider carefully. Ham, in this story, represents the threatening international situation that you live in." That Ham might have more sons besides Canaan is not mentioned here. Other sons do appear in Genesis 10 within the "table of nations." But in Genesis 9 Ham has only one son, Canaan. The curse of servitude was laid on the Canaanites, then, *not* because of Ham's sins, but because of their *own* sins, which were probably analogous to Ham's sin related in the story of Noah.

Cursing and blessing never work in a cause and effect nexus in the Bible. They function dynamically within the poles of sin and judgment, of grace and conversion. For this reason, the Canaanite people were not *permanently* shut off from the blessing Abraham was to bring to the families of the earth. The better possibility for Canaan comes out early in the Old Testament. When Rahab, the Canaanite woman, moves out in trust to Israel and Israel's God, she finds the hands of blessing and is eventually honored as one of the ancestors of Jesus, the son of Abraham (see Josh. 1, Matt. 1, and Heb. 11). Tamar, another Canaanite, also is listed in the genealogical tables of Jesus, a living demonstration that Jesus the Messiah had come for sinners, and for all peoples, including the Canaanites.

When Jesus' disciples wanted to call down fire from heaven, as when it rained down on the Canaanites in Sodom and Gomorrah and on the Canaanite priests of Baal at Mt. Carmel, Jesus put His foot down. He had not come to curse and to destroy. He had come to save. Luke adds that Jesus rebuked the disciples for their vindictive urge (Luke 9:51-56).

Surely, it has to be clear that the manipulations of this Genesis passage to defend slavery or to burden the Negroid peoples with an inherited curse of inferiority, belong among the ugliest forms of pseudo-theologies ever devised. That they could persist so long demonstrates anew that men as well as demons can manipulate the Bible to justify their manipulations of people.

It may help bury this particular piece of pseudo-theology if we summarize a few important features of the Genesis 9 passage:

(1) The writer of Genesis 9 had no intention of including other Hamites, along with Canaan, in the temporary curse spoken over Canaan. And no other Canaanites are involved in the curse than the ones Israel encountered as adversaries in the land of Canaan.

(2) The identification of the biblical Hamites with a specific race (the Negroids) is based on an obvious misconception. The designation "Canaan, the son of Ham" does not point to a racial distinction at all, but to a political and geographical situation in the second millen-

nium before Christ, when the Canaanites were vassals of the Pharaoh and so for this reason are counted among the Hamites.

(3) As far as their biological origin and their language are concerned, the Canaanites belong among the *Semites*. Just as there are no racial distinctions but only political-geographical distinctions in the "table of nations' of Genesis 10, there are no racial overtones to Genesis 9.

(4) The term *Hamitic* is not used in modern science to indicate a particular *race*; it is used only for a general language-group, one to which the Egyptians, among others, belong. (See *The New Bible Dictionary*, ed. J. D. Douglas [Grand Rapids, Mich., 1962], under "Ham.") *There is no Hamitic race.*

(5) Cause and effect from generation to generation do not figure in Genesis 9. The Canaanites do not suffer for the guilt of Ham, and are not victims of a disadvantaged inheritance. They suffer for their *own* sins, and the same way to forgiveness and conversion is open to them as it is to all others.

With this we conclude our excursion into what is basically irrelevant to the subject, and can now go on to listen to the biblical message about the relationship between races.

SOLIDARITY IN GUILT

The Bible talks not only of the vanity of the human race, and of the variety that blossoms within this unity, but also of human unity in guilt, of solidarity in sin. The Bible tells us what we are, and does it with confident authority. All people and all races are swept up in a collective rebellion against God and one another. Paul lets the searchlight of God's Law play over all the peoples of the world, Jews and Gentiles alike, in Romans 3. There, he comes to this unsettling conclusion: "For all have sinned and fallen short of the glory of God" (vss.

10,12,23). Every people and every race play their part in the guilt that haunts the world. All peoples walk in darkness.

"All flesh is grass, and all its beauty is like the flower of the field. The grass withers, the flower fades, when the breath of the Lord blows upon it; surely the people is grass" (Isa. 40:6,7). The same book of Genesis that tells us about man's noble beginning also tells us about his fall. First, communication with God (Gen. 3) is broken, then the bond between man and man, brother and brother (the story of Cain and Abel). The centrifugal force that sends group away from group and race from race quickly becomes visible. It is profoundly dramatized in the well-known story of the tower of Babel (Gen. 11). A society takes collective initiative against God. "Come, let us build ourselves a city, and a tower with its top in the heavens, and let us make a name for ourselves, lest we be scattered abroad upon the face of the whole earth." In this story, the motives that move men toward the building of human society and at the same time pervert it to the hilt are all exposed.

What are the motives behind this collective initiative?

First, there is a decision to secede from the living God. We see here a collective movement to make a massive defense against God. Fear of the living God drives them together, as animals close ranks when they smell danger in the wind. "Come," they say, "let us collectively resign from obedience to God, let us force His abdication and dethronement and establish ourselves secure forever against the invasion of His judgment."

Secondly, they are driven by a fear and distrust of one another. The same thing is seen everywhere in the world; where God is dethroned, people are delivered to a deep distrust of one another. Where God does not rule, there are no more norms that matter, no more divine commands that obligate. Each is delivered to his own instincts and egotistic drives. No one can predict how the other is going to act. One group no longer is sure how the other group is going to respond. Where divine norms are absent, everything becomes unpredictable. Where there is no magnetic center, all sorts of centrifugal forces go to work. Where the vertical line, the relationship to God, is broken, the horizontal line is also distorted. The people back there, in the plains of Mesopotamia, experienced this fact, and it has been felt in every phase of the history of culture. This accounts for the demonic initiative for defensive consolidation. "Come, let us hold on to each other, lest we be spread out over the earth. Come, let none hold back, let us all close ranks in a massive opposition against the living God. Come, let no one sabotage our unity here in the flatlands of Shinar. Our thoughts, our wills, our words must melt together in one battle-cry: Unity is power!"

A third motive is self-deification. Having decided to dethrone God, they also decide to exalt themselves in a collective titanism. A voice whispers to an individual in Genesis 3: "You shall be as gods." But in Genesis 11, the voice cries aloud, a demonic voice from the masses: "Come, let us collectively exalt ourselves as gods. Let us build temple towers like the towers of the gods so that we can inhabit them ourselves as gods. Let us storm heaven with our tower, undo the gods that be, and take their places. Come, let us raise a collective anthem to our own power, our own name, our own glory, our own plans, our own thoughts, our own counsel, and our own deeds."

Thus a tower arose in Babel, like a clenched fist directed against the living God. It was a symbol of human self-glorification and self-deification, a collective effort to organize the world without God, and thus to make a name for men.

The story is a window on all human history. Studying the relationship among the races, we discover the same forces—fear of God, fear of one another, and the urge to self-deification (making a name for one's self). This is why it never works to create a society in our own power.

We seek unity and we find division; we seek harmony and find discord; we seek peace and find war; we seek consolidation and find bifurcation. We want to be gods, self-made gods, but we end up as devils.

This is why associations between peoples and races look more like a macro-chaos than they do a macro-cosmos; we build not on the New Jerusalem, the city of peace, but on Babel, the city of confusion. The tower of Babel is not only a window on the centrifugal forces that drive societal life apart. It is also a window on God's judgment. But, and this is important, it also reveals God's plan to *restore* fellowship of life among the nations and races.

God comes down, we read in Genesis 11, to inspect the city's bulwarks. And He drives the builders in all directions. The inner confusion that was implicit from the beginning now explodes into explicit view. God spreads the builders out over the earth and leaves them to migrate to their own places. The tower is buried in the cemetery of human expectations. The city becomes wasteland; the jackals take over. The monument to human pride becomes a monument to human scandal. In this way, God's judgment touches down on man's efforts to build a society without Him. The thunder of His judgment still echoes through history. But it is not empty of grace. The negative message of Genesis 11 does not cancel out the positive message of unity within diversity that the "table of nations" proclaims. God's purpose has not shifted, as though it now aims at human apartheid. His intent is to manifest the unity of the peoples in Him. His plan is not to cause the disintegration of societal life, but to save it.

He has no wish to disperse; He seeks to gather. If the peoples split off from one another because each group, isolated from the others, wants to make a name for its own language, its own race—this only spurs God on to restore them to one another, to do everything that has to be done to that end. He aims to bring about a *new* unity where the name of the Lord is a strong tower, where everyone who calls on His name will find the way back to the secret of genuine humanity—life with God and with one another in unbreakable fellowship. This is what the election of Israel is all about, and this is what the ministry of Jesus Christ is all about.

Before going into this more deeply, we should pull together a few conclusions from what the Bible tells us about the solidarity of all races in guilt.

(1) All races and ethnic groups share in the guilt men bear over against God and one another. In all parts of the world, from prehistoric times until now, men have shared in pride, self-deification, titanism, fear, and distrust of one another. Everywhere and always these sins against God and neighbor have erupted into conflict, murderous hostility, and both personal and collective egoism. In modern times groups, classes, and races have discovered more effective methods and techniques to exploit their sinfulness; but from the earliest periods of human life, history is laced with pride and poisoned with egoism. In whatever part of the world we live, we have all sinned and spoiled the glory of God (Rom. 3).

(2) There are no superior races. No people and no race has any right to consider itself superior or to consider another inferior. There are no noble races who have a reason to look on others as ignoble. Before God all peoples and all races have lost their nobility.

(3) The temptation in every group to make a scapegoat of other groups and so to excuse itself from guilt, is evidence of collective pride, and only increases one's own guilt.

(4) Every man, every group, every nation and every race must learn through God's spirit to confess humbly its share in the common guilt of the world. True renewal in race relations will come about only as every race recognizes that it walks in darkness and then learns to listen to the words of Isaiah: "Arise, shine; for your light has come, and the glory of the Lord has risen upon

you. . . . And nations shall come to your light, and kings
to the brightness of your rising" (Isa. 60:1,3).

ISRAEL'S ELECTION AND THE BLESSING
OF THE NATIONS

We have seen that one of the core themes of the Old
Testament is the unity of the human family and the
grateful surprise at the variations in which the unity
comes to expression. We have also noted the solidarity in
guilt that burdens all peoples and at the same time
summons them to liberation, redemption, restoration,
peace, and reconciliation. This is the background we must
keep in view as we discuss the election of Israel. Israel is
chosen and called with a view to the nations. "In you,"
God says to Abraham, "shall all the nations of the earth
be blessed."

Temporarily, Israel, the people of Abraham, is separated from the nations (Ex. 19:3ff.; Deut. 7:14ff.) so
that a relation between Jahweh and Israel could be established that would prepare the way for the realization of
God's plan of liberation for all the nations. The wall that
separated Israel and the nations was not meant to be a
permanent dividing wall. It served only to preserve this
one people, in the midst of the nations, until the time
came to break down the wall of division and to reveal to
all nations the secret of God's liberating plan. There is
not a trace of racism in God's election of Israel. Israel is
chosen, but as *pars pro toto*—a part for the whole—with
an eye to all other nations, a minority in the service of
the majority. Nothing at all of a Herrenvolk is suggested.
Precisely the contrary. As clearly as possible, the Old
Testament stresses that Israel was not called because of
any superior qualities it might claim to possess; it was
called although this puny group of wandering Arameans
had no such qualities (Deut. 7:7; Ezek. 16:3-15). Israel
had nothing to boast of. It was purely an object of God's
mercy, its identity and destiny were defined wholly by

God's saving plans to make Israel a people of the cove‑
nant. Israel was chosen to be the vehicle of God's saving
revelation, a revelation directed at all the nations. Jahweh
is not a tribal god, but the God of all nations, and He
associates Himself freely with Israel, as its Covenant-God,
only to prepare and actualize His salvation for all others.

The prophets of Israel had to keep struggling with false
prophets who, diametrically against God's will, tried to
turn Israel into a Herrenvolk, to exploit aspects of Israel's
life as tokens of superiority, and turn Jahweh into a tribal
god so that He too could be exploited for their own
purposes. C. J. Labuschagne writes, "No other nation in
the world has, with so much care, preserved writings that
uttered so critical, sometimes shattering, a judgment a‑
gainst its own people and its own religion." Working from
this observation, he concentrates on the latent conflict
between the true and the false prophets that erupted in
moments of crisis. What was the core of the conflict
between Micaiah and Zedekiah the son of Chenaanah (I
Kings 22), between Jeremiah and Hananiah, between
Amos and the temple prophets, to name just a few?
Labuschagne has shown that the core of the conflict lay
here, that the pseudo-prophets introduced an ethnocen‑
tric, nationalist political religiosity, a pseudo‑Jahwism, in
which the religious traditions were distorted into tribal-
myths. In the tribal-ideology of the false prophets, Jah‑
weh was seen as a tribal, revelation was replaced by
nationalist slogans, the Torah traded for a chauvinistic
tribal-will, the cult misused as a magical-nationalistic ritu‑
al in order to secure the safety of the people (see Jer.
7:10). This religiosity was racist, ethnocentric, and anti-
ecumenical, and it fostered national pride; in it Israel
began to preen itself as "the first of the nations" (Amos
6:1). It is against this racism that the true prophets
thundered the judgment of God. In their wrestling with
pseudo-Jahwism and racist tribal-ideology, the prophets
also talked about a new order that would come; in the
middle of these serious crisis situations, they talked of

the salvation of Jahweh that would reveal the glory of the Lord to all peoples (Isa. 60). In those critical situations, they proclaimed that Jahweh was not a tribal god, and that the temporary theocracy of the Old Testament was going to disappear before the universal Messianic Kingdom of God, who would rule "from sea to sea, and from the River to the ends of the earth!" (Ps. 72:8; see also Isa. 45:22; Jer. 10:1-6; Zech. 14:9,16; Ps. 47:3,8).

Thus, the Old Testament often points beyond itself to a new era in which the temporary wall of separation between Israel and the nations would be broken down for good, and in which the purpose of God's revelation to Israel would be fulfilled by the Messiah, Jesus, in whom and through whom the peace and salvation of God would be brought to all the nations of the world.

Summarizing, we may say that the only distinction the Bible makes between peoples is that between Israel and the nations. This distinction, however, has nothing at all to do with racism or ethnocentrism, even though it was distorted in that fashion by Israel. This distinction had a place in God's worldwide redemption plan. It was temporary and intended only to serve these plans, and is, finally, abandoned in the coming of Jesus Christ (see Eph. 2:14-16).

JESUS HAS BROKEN DOWN THE WALL

We have considered the fundamental unity of the human family, the variety of races, and the solidarity of all peoples and races in man's communal rebellion against God and neighbor. These, we saw, are central to the whole matter of race relations. But they are not the last word the Bible speaks. The Bible proclaims good news, the good news for the relationship between races. It is the message of peace and reconciliation through Jesus Christ the Lord, through Him who reconciles men and peoples with God and with one another. This is the good news that Jesus Christ has broken down the wall that divided people and races from one another. We cannot, within the limits of this book, possibly do justice to the significance of Jesus Christ for our subject. But we must say something. First, we will take a few close-ups from the Gospels to illustrate His significance by way of some specific data and stories.

A. The Genealogy of Jesus

Matthew 1 gives us the remarkable family line of Jesus. Kohlbrugge has described this family register as the ladder down which Jesus climbed into human history. What is remarkable about the genealogy is that it emphasizes not only that Jesus came to us via sinners, but that He came down through a variety of nations and races. Four women from non-Israelitic peoples appear in the register: Tamar and Rahab (both Canaanites), Ruth (a Moabite), and Bathsheba (a Hittite). These names appear in the genealogy to proclaim that Jesus came not only for Israel, but for all nations.

B. Jesus' Encounter with Non-Israelites

We will mention only a few stories that illustrate Jesus' attitude toward non-Israelite outsiders.

The meeting between Jesus and the Samaritan woman is one of the most moving stories of the Gospels (John 4). Jewish custom had set up an impassable race barrier between Jews and Samaritans. But Jesus totally ignores the barrier. This Samaritan woman is one of the first to whom Jesus reveals His Messianic secret. In a conversation that bores deeply into the mystery of His identity, He proffers living water that saves and heals her. When her fellow townspeople come, Jesus reveals Himself to the folk of Sychar as the Liberator and Savior; and they gratefully acknowledge that in Him they have found the Savior of the world (John 4:42). The text actually has it that they found Him to be "Liberator of the cosmos."

So, at the very beginning of John's Gospel, the cosmic and universal significance of Jesus is illumined. The same loving concern for people from other races is seen in Jesus' encounter with the Syrophoenician woman. Jesus finds Himself in "heathen territory," beyond the limits of Israel (Mark 7:24-30). The woman He meets is a heathen, but He reveals His Savior's heart to her and her daughter. The whole story vibrates with the holy impatience Jesus has while He limits Himself temporarily to the lost sheep of the house of Israel and all the while longs for the day when salvation would be turned loose toward the other peoples. We find still another example of Jesus' universal concern in the story of the Roman centurion (Matt. 8:8-10). Here is a man who recognizes that he needs help for himself and his family, and Jesus does not hesitate to be a Savior, a Liberator, for him.

Perhaps the most remarkable of Jesus' encounters with the "others, strangers from afar," is His meeting with the Greek deputation, related in John 12:20-36. The shadow of the Cross has already begun to fall over Jesus' life. He knows that He is going to be thrown into the earth as a mustard seed, to die and rise again. At that moment, some Greeks present a proposition to Him, perhaps a proposal for Him to escape Palestine and flee to Greece. Jesus' answer to the Greeks, and to us all, is this: "And I, when I am lifted up from the earth, will draw all men to myself" (John 12:32). With these words, Jesus points to the universal significance of His death and resurrection, a significance that would be proclaimed and experienced among all men. He reveals, at the same time, that He would be the Reconciler of the nations. He is not only an example for us; He not only illustrates what neighbor love is like. He does not merely embody as an object lesson what love for people of every race means. He is also the one who bears God's judgment on the broken communication between peoples and races and the one who has restored the communication for us.

C. *The Excommunicated Jesus Restores Communication*

Jesus died *for* us all—so the Bible tells us. But He also died at the hands of us all. The legal murder of the Holy Lord implicates us all. Through Caiaphas, who represented Israel, through Pilate, who represented Rome, we excommunicated Jesus. The bloody cry "Crucify Him" carried overtones of our voices; we helped lead Him outside the gate and nail Him to the cross.

He who died at the hands of all of us, died for all of us. He bore, in those three hours of God-forsakenness, God's judgment on our broken communication. He who lived heartbeat by heartbeat in communication with God and man, landed there, in desolate loneliness, with all communication broken. See the Lamb of God who took away the sins of the world. There, at the cross, where communication is broken, that is where communication is restored forever through His obedience. Above His head is written an inscription—in Hebrew, the language of religion; in Latin, the language of justice and statehood; in Greek, the language of culture. All men, all peoples, can now know that there is mercy through Him, even for the horrible sins committed in race relations. All nations and races may and must now know that there is forgiveness, and that reconciliation has come, and that a basis has been laid for a new fellowship of men.

His body was broken and His blood shed for a complete remission of the sins committed in our race relations. And His resurrection proclaims a new beginning, the restoration of humanity, a new communion of men.

D. *The Implications of Jesus' Life, Death, and Resurrection for Race Relations*

Paul's letters spell out the significance of Jesus' life, death, and resurrection. And they give us deep insights into the race question.

1. JESUS HAS TAKEN ON HUMAN NATURE FOR ALL RACES

Jesus is God-with-us and man-with-us. Paul calls Him the second Adam, the representative of the whole human family. He has taken on human *nature*, as the ecumenical creeds put it. This son of Israel, this child of Mary, has assumed to Himself all humanity. The humanity of all, without discrimination, was taken on in the Incarnation of the Son of God. And so He has to do with all men, and is bound to all men.

He who despises, hates, discriminates against other races, does the same to Jesus. It applies to anti-semitism; he who despises the Jew despises Jesus. But it works all the way—for whites, for blacks, for yellow, for brown; he who hates, despises, demeans, any or all of them hates Jesus. This is why the declaration of Uppsala was so right; racism is a denial of faith in Christ.

2. JESUS BROKE DOWN THE WALL THAT SEPARATED THE RACES IN ORDER TO RESTORE THE UNITY OF MAN

Paul speaks of this in Ephesians 2:11-22, especially in verses 14-16, from which I have borrowed the title of this book. I will cite verses 14-16:

> For he is our peace, who has made us both one, and has broken down the wall of hostility, by abolishing in his flesh the law of commandments and ordinances, that he might create in himself one new man in place of the two, so making peace, and might reconcile us both to God in one body through the cross, thereby bringing the hostility to an end.

The point of the hymn is to sing the praises of God's liberating actions in Christ. God's purpose in Christ is to establish peace between Himself and men and among men themselves. Peace is real when men live together with

Him in communal fellowship. This purpose is illustrated first by what God has done and is doing in Christ for the relationship between Jew and Gentile. The *ethnē*, the peoples, mean all non-Jewish people. Between Jew and Gentile there stood a wall, as a temporary ordinance of God. The Old Testament prophets repeatedly promised that this wall of division would one day become obsolete and be broken down (Isa. 5:5; 60). The coming of Jesus signals the wall's definite obsolescence. The separation between the "far and the near" is overcome. Jesus, the Jew from Nazareth, crucified by both Jew and Gentile, reconciled both in one body even while He abandoned Himself to their common hostilities. The wall is abandoned. A new time has broken in. The Lord is risen. Out goes a summons to the Gentiles; they are no longer shut out. Out goes a summons to the Jews; they are no longer to cut themselves off from other people.

What God did and is doing in the relationship between the Jews and the *goyim* illustrates that His purpose is to break down all walls between all men, in and through Jesus Christ, and to make of humanity one whole, one body. Jesus Christ—as is indicated everywhere in Ephesians—is the Head of a new humanity. In Him God wants to integrate men and nations. Now the church, according to this passage and several others in the same letter, is the avant-garde of this integration; it is the integration center. The church must be seen as a tentative manifestation of the restored unity and universality of the whole human family.

We could say that Ephesians summarizes the biblical message to us about the relationship of the races. What must not be missed is the way the church is brought into this liberating process that involves God Himself in bringing the humanity of man into revelation as a single body. It is the church's job to be a servant of this process. It must be a sign in human history of authentic reintegration.

This has profound and broad implications for us. If it

is true that the time of the veil that covered God's Law is now forever in the past, then it is also the time for lifting all the other veils, behind which human fears, human prohibitions, human powers have hid. The church of Christ has the calling to translate God's purpose for man. In the church of Christ, no people, no race is excluded, and in the church we are called to join the struggle to remove all segregating veils. God's command now resounds against every wall of division, and those who are disciples of Christ are shoved out into the world to obey this command in the church and in society.

In South Africa, I was criticized for twisting the message of Ephesians into a "social gospel." I was told that I had managed only to substitute my own "integration-theology" for the "apartheid-ideology" that I condemned. But I would like to allow the message of Ephesians to press this question on us: Do we really preach the Gospel if the Gospel we preach has no implications for our social existence? And if, as Ephesians insists, it is the will of God to reintegrate mankind, what would come of our faithfulness to His message if we soft-pedaled or sabotaged that part?

To conclude this section, I should like to refer to Markus Barth's brilliant book on Ephesians, *The Broken Wall.* At the close of his remarks on that part of Ephesians which we have discussed above, Barth says something like this: The many facets of meaning in the broken wall give us not only the right, but the obligation to recognize in the wall more than the strictly religious sides of individual lives. To confess Christ is to witness to the conquest of separation, segregation, apartheid, and of all ghettoes. We build all sorts of walls to serve as barriers between people and races, but our comfort is this: none of these walls has any status with God. God's work in Christ cannot be undone. He has in fact integrated humanity. That is the structure of His work. And we are called in His Spirit to continue the work. It is meaningless to acknowledge Christ as Lord unless we honor Him as the creator of the new humanity and as the end of all segregation. In the words of Ephesians itself: "For we are his workmanship, created in Christ Jesus for good works, which God prepared beforehand that we should walk in them" (Eph. 2:10). The basic task of breaking down the walls is finished. Jesus did it. We don't have to do it again. What has to happen now is for us to set out from that reality and to walk in that Spirit.

The Gospel according to Ephesians 2 and 3 is an anthem to the work of Jesus—the demolition of the wall of hostility and the reintegration of humanity. Now that Christ has broken down the wall and prepared the way for man to become one man, anyone trying to build the wall up again is a saboteur. The job now is to be co-workers with God in the spread of His integration policy.

THE SPIRIT-CREATED COMMUNITY

Redemption through Jesus Christ offers a fundamental restoration of the fellowship between men of all races. The Holy Spirit, the Spirit of the Father who created all men in countless varieties and the Spirit of the Son who redeemed the nations, is the Spirit who restores the fellowship within the daily realities of life as both a gift and a command.

To say that He restores communication as a gift is to say that the fellowship between peoples of all nations is a *given*, a profound reality that cannot be undone by human shortsightedness, arrogance, or pride. When we say that the Holy Spirit restores communication as a command, as a calling and a commission, we mean that the Holy Spirit commissions us to take on ourselves, as our responsibility and task, the fellowship that Christ created and that the Holy Spirit promises to preserve and expand. This is the way the Bible often talks to us: What God gives as a gift comes as a challenge. Let us pick a few classic examples of this out of the New Testament.

We can begin with the sending of the Holy Spirit at

Pentecost (Acts 2). That was surely an interracial experience. On that day in Jerusalem, Jews were present from every country to which they had been dispersed. But proselytes were there too, non-Jewish people who had assumed the Jewish religion. Acts 2 lists the places they had come from, and they include areas in Asia, Africa, and Europe. They heard "the great deeds of God" proclaimed, they heard what Jesus of Nazareth had done and would do to reconcile men of all nations with God and with one another. And while they listened, the Holy Spirit began to operate in many hearts; thousands were "filled with the Holy Spirit" and entered the fellowship of those who had discovered reconciliation with God and with each other. Among the many miracles that happened there, two are most instructive for us here.

The story of Pentecost lies at the opposite pole from the story of Babel. At Babel, language, the instrument of communication, became the instrument of confusion and diversion. At Pentecost, the Gospel of reconciliation was preached in several languages, but language at that moment became the instrument of a new community. The history of Babel's tower shows us centrifugal forces driving races and peoples apart. The story of Pentecost shows us people from very many different nations finding each other around the Center, the Savior of the world. The language barrier falls—and the race barrier falls at the same time.

One of the most remarkable events in the early Christian congregation is the fellowship experienced in the church at Jerusalem by people of different races. Arabs and Jews and Turks are members of the same fellowship. Babylonians, Syrians, and blacks join hands in the same gatherings but also experience communion with one another outside the church services and away from the Lord's table. Romans, Greeks, Asians, and Africans practiced authentic brotherly fellowship without restrictions. As every point on the circumference has the same relationship to the center of the circle, these people fellow-shiped with God and with each other through their common relationship with the Center, Jesus Christ. This was true in Jerusalem, but it also happened both as gift and command in many other early Christian communities. One can read the names of the leading figures in the congregation at Antioch (Acts 13) and discover the names of Negroes, Jews, Edomites, Greeks, and others. No doubt some congregations were made up almost wholly of Jewish Christians, and others overwhelmingly of Gentile Christians. But there was no congregation that existed exclusively of a single ethnic group. And it is also clear that these congregations exercised brotherhood and fellowship in ways, both with words and actions, that created tensions in the pagan environment. Paul was the man who became the champion for a completely multi-racial church concept. He carried on a life-long struggle in pursuit of his vision of the broken wall and never com-promised. He could not compromise because he knew that the Christian faith stood or fell with it. His multi-racial concept was accepted at the apostle's synod of Acts 15. Even Simon Peter went along with it, after his lesson in Christian integration on Simon's roof in Joppa (Acts 10).

Paul works out his conception into many nuances. The most famous expressions are found in Colossians 3:10,11, Galatians 3:28, and Ephesians 2:14 and 22. But in all his letters he urges his readers to put away the old man with his evil practices. And the practices he mentions have much to do with racism—despising other men and groups, pride, wrath, discrimination, and so on. And the readers are cajoled to put on the new man. What is the typical demeanor of the new humanity that reflects the image of Christ? Its characteristic is that in it there is no such thing as Jew or Greek, slave or free, male or female, barbarian or Scythian, but only the one man in Christ. The point is clear: All these differences have lost their decisive, divi-

sion-creating meaning, lost it radically, and whoever acts
as though these differences are decisive, division-creating
differences, has in fact denied Christ.

Anyone who knows anything at all about the tensions
between racial groups senses how Paul's warning hits the
question of race relations at dead center. In Colossians
3:13,14 we find a summons to be kind, humble, and
forgiving toward one another. We find the task given us
to forgive each other and to be patient with one another,
the task of talking out the complaints that one man has
against another until they are resolved, the task to live in
peace with one another for Christ's sake.

In Galatians 5 and Ephesians 2, we meet the same
message and the same task. The New Testament letters do
not merely summon us to effect this restored fellowship
within the church. We are also called to spread the
renewing influence felt within the church out into the life
of society in general. Max Warren points out in his book
on Galatians (*The Gospel of Victory*) that its urgings
must be read against the background of the very compli-
cated multiracial social life in Galatia. Peter's letters
suggest a similar background. They were written to Christians in Asia Minor, a small minority in the midst of a
national conglomeration. Peter, himself schooled in the
academy of Jesus Christ, notes how in this sort of interracial society the relationships between people can be
poisoned by jealousy, anger, and rumor between the
groups and how people often look for scapegoats for
their troubles and carry on intrigues and gossip campaigns
against each other. He calls the disciples of Jesus to resist
the influence of this atmosphere and to demonstrate their
own reality as a new people, a people gathered from all
ethnic groups, "a holy nation, God's own people." Then
he tells these people, living in the midst of that tense,
hostile society, to be led by gentleness, truth, friendliness, love, and patience. In this way, by their way of life
amid racial tensions, they would proclaim the great work
of Him who called us out of darkness into His wonderful
light (I Pet. 1-4).

THE CELEBRATION OF FELLOWSHIP WITH GOD
AND BROTHERHOOD BETWEEN RACES

The Bible does more than speak of the person and work of Christ as Redeemer and Peacemaker, more than speak of the restored fellowship which is manifest among those who truly let the Spirit lead them. The Bible also promises that this restored fellowship will one day be perfectly realized. The writings of the apostles and prophets are charged to the limit with this future reality, this eschatological promise that bears so meaningfully on us.

The Bible contains a protology, a message about the first things, from which the unity of the human race and its solidarity in guilt is drawn (Gen. 1-11). But it also contains an eschatology, a teaching of the last things, in which the "first things shall be done away" and in which all relationships are set right. The language in which this comes to us is visionary and symbolic. The Second Letter of Peter speaks of the disappearance of the structures of injustice (including racial injustice) and of the "new heaven and new earth in which justice shall dwell." That this justice implies a new state of affairs in race relations is worked out for us in the visionary language of the book of Revelation.

In this apocalyptic language, all that was begun in Jesus Christ is extrapolated and becomes an encouraging catalyst for us. The struggle for racial justice is not in vain, and the victory is assured. In Revelation 21 this promise is cloaked in the image of the New Jerusalem. Here is God's metropolis, God's ecumenopolis, the center of the new order, the center of the new heaven and the new earth. With profuse imagery, we are told that the foundation stones of the city carry the names of the apostles of the Lamb. That is, the fellowship within this metropolis rests on the person and work of Jesus Christ. The gates of the city are open to all corners of the earth, to South and East and North and West. People from all corners of the earth come through the Northern gate, the

Southern gate, the Western gate, and the Eastern gate.
Together they become the citizens, the political fellowship of the ecumenopolis. They celebrate together the
feast of fellowship with God, for the glory of God lights
this city, and the "Lamb is their lamp." They also celebrate the feast of unbroken brotherhood between people
of all nations and races. The people walk together in the
light of God, and the kings of the earth lay their glory
down within the city (Rev. 21:9-24). This is what is
really festive about the festival; the people will really
serve God and each other forever. This symbolic vision
with which the Bible closes is given to us so that we, in
our present history, will be obedient to it. Apocalyptic
fragments from the Bible are often used as an opium of
the people, as an escape from responsibility in the here
and now, as a dispensation from the task of today. But
biblical apocalyptic is not meant as a drug. It is meant as
a tonic to stimulate us to join the struggle for racial
justice.

God wills that lines be drawn connecting our situation
and the New Jerusalem to come, in the area of race
relations as well as in others. If we live out of the same
sources from which come our racism and our racial dis-
harmony, we are not living in contact with the New
Jerusalem, the city of peace and righteousness. Those
who live with their roots in the reconciliation won by
Christ are called into the service of reconciliation, to be
party-members with Christ in the struggle against all
racial injustice. The festival of fellowship with God and
the brotherhood of the races are going to come. He who
wants to celebrate must join in the preparations for it
that are now taking place.

Those who, in the relationship between races, wear the
stamp of Cain, and of the Beast and of Babel, the city of
titanism and chaos, will be shut out of the festival.
Joining the celebration will be all who, here, in the daily
affairs of the city, live by the Lamb in restored fellowship
with God and men.

We have tried, very briefly, to present the promises and demands in the Bible relevant to the relationship of the races. The principal resistance against hostility and segregation between the races lies in simple obedience to the Good News. This has enormous point in our time. It may be significant that organizations like UNESCO, assisted by experts from several areas, devote themselves to the struggle against racial injustice. Without doubt, this sort of action has great value. But it is an illusion to suppose that "science and reason" are enough to bring healing into race relations.

A century ago, Darwin predicted that we would bring about better relationships between peoples and races through "science and reason." But, as Visser 't Hooft has remarked, the facts unfortunately provide no support for Darwin's optimism. Why? Why cannot "reason and science" ever make a real and fundamental difference in such issues as the race question? It is because this kind of question is decided in the depths of human nature. The healing of relations between races is achieved only through rebirth, through radical conversion. The Holy Spirit Himself must bring about renewal and change. Even knowing what the Bible says is not in itself going to lead automatically to obedience to God's Word. The Pharisees and scribes are classic examples of people who were "armed with knowledge of the Word" but who sabotaged it in practice. And in Nazi Germany theologians and princes of the church, too, were bought off to betray the teaching of Christ about the relationship between the races. All the water of the oceans cannot wash away this fact, that changes in the relationship between races can begin only as people and groups are personally and structurally converted to obedience to God's Gospel and God's Law.

Now that we have reflected on what the Bible has to say about race relations, we must go on to look at the practical consequences of all this for the situation the world now finds itself in.

Chapter Three

Imperialism and Racism

Now we must set foot in the reality of our own situation, where *we* are summoned to obey what the Bible tells us about the relationship of the races. This means, in the first instance, that we are called to *join* the struggle against injustice, and that we are called to seek out the righteousness of the Kingdom of God in the context of race relations. We want in this chapter to devote ourselves to the general causes of the disturbances in race relations and to wait until the next chapter to consider territories and situations in which the struggle is now more urgent than ever.

THE STRUGGLE AGAINST RACISM

One of the most agitated springs from which injustices in race relations flow is the spiritual power we have learned to call *racism*. Racism, as we see it, means the pride that one racial group has in reference to another, the exclusive approval of the customs and characteristics of one's own group and the negative, stand-offish feelings that one group has towards other racial groups, together with the tendency of each group's members to discriminate against and to cut off members of another group from full participation in the life of society.

Racism is a very old thing. It appears in the family-pride, tribal-pride, and clan-pride of ancient times. The

56

remarkable thing about our time is racism's cosmopolitan appearance.

Racism expresses itself in concrete structures, some of which we must talk about frankly in the next chapter. Here, we are concerned especially with the root from which racism grows. Jesus told the parable of the Pharisee and the publican to tell us about people who justify themselves and despise other people (Luke 18:9-14). What Jesus says about individuals here holds for groups as well. Racism is collective Pharisaism; and collective Pharisaism is as real as are individual Pharisees.

Racism has many faces. It comes out in demeaning gossip about other groups. It pops up when one's pride is pricked and he responds with resentment against other groups. It gets structured in the formation, building, and buttressing of racial prejudice. One of the most striking forms of racism is the tendency to make scapegoats of others. As the collective dreams of one group are frustrated by tough reality, the collective urge to self-preservation tempts people to find other people to blame for their disappointment.

The most gruesome example of the scapegoat ploy was the case of National Socialism. The Jews were made scapegoats in Germany, and the collective willingness to massacre the Jews was its natural climax. But scapegoat devices are found everywhere. Whenever various ethnic groups live in the same environment with other ethnic groups, one finds the scapegoat syndrome. Collective human nature creates an irresistible urge in groups to burden other groups for mistakes that they have made themselves. Jesus calls us to struggle against all forms of pride, and includes racism in them. He said that anyone who exalts himself and demeans another shall himself be demeaned. And anyone who humbles himself shall be exalted. This must be true of societies as well as of individuals.

Within the main racial groups there is a vigorous force toward racism among the subgroups. Relations between

Frenchmen and Germans have long been infected with ethnic pride; racism is a threat to relations between the Ibos and the Hausas, between the Tamils and the Singhalese, between the Chinese and the Polynesians. Our present world is full of inter-ethnic and inter-tribal tensions. But the most virulent form of racism has been, and in many respects still is, white racism; the other forms of racism are in many instances (for example, in the United States) a kind of counter-racism, and function as a protective reaction to white racism.

What is the antidote against racism? The Bible constantly calls us to do battle against injustice, but it is just as serious in its summons to justice. The antidote against racism is given by Jesus Christ in the so-called Golden Rule found in the Sermon on the Mount: "So whatever you wish that men would do to you, do so to them; for this is the law and the prophets" (Matt. 7:12). In other words, "You want to be treated without discrimination, then treat others without discrimination." "You want people of other races to treat you as an equal, then treat them as equals." "You want the other groups to respond to you in a loving and friendly way, then treat them in a loving and friendly way." "You want others not to be vengeful towards you, but to forgive you and make a new start with you, then begin by forgiving them." "You want others to understand your particular situation, your problems, then treat others in sympathy with their situation, their position, their problems." This is the antidote against racism.

The Golden Rule is so simple; nothing could be easier to grasp. Its application, however, comes hard; nothing seems harder to practice. And yet its burden is light and its yoke is easy if we live in the power of Him who applied the same rule in His own life and death, and who goes on in the history of the resurrection age empowering people to live by it.

UNMASKING RACIAL MYTHS

Equality and harmony in race relations demand the unmasking of racial myths and bogus racial theories. The job of exposure is unending in the struggle against racial injustice and for racial justice.

What are racial myths? In ancient tribal religions, the group projected its inner thought and feeling world into a whole complex of myths. The thoughts were not formulated in concepts and theories, but in images and stories. An ancient society used its tribal myths to project its thoughts and feelings about its own origin, value, greatness, glory, and destiny. We cannot, of course, within the scope of our study, go into the details of the various myths. Nor is it necessary: they all tell essentially the same story. It is the proud story of how the ur-ancestors of the tribe were a *divine* couple, of how the descendants of these gods formed a very special generation of men, a generation of sons and daughters of the gods, and of how these gave birth to a tribe of men with whom no other tribes can possibly be compared. The tribal myths are always a case of tribal self-adoration. The myths are the reflection of a tribe's own feelings of self-exaltation. In its myths, the tribe expresses its collective pride.

Tribal myths are not an extinct art. They reappear in new forms constantly and will not die as long as men are alive. One of the conclusions to which the study of religions leads is that mythological thinking is not limited to a particular phase of history, as Auguste Comte figured, but is built into the human mode of experiencing its own life. They are most resilient. They have not been done in by enlightenment or science, and for a simple reason: progress and science cannot touch the basic characteristics of the human heart. We have had a horrible education in this fact within our time. Japanese Shintoism forced us to look hard into a tribal myth, a

myth that intoxicated the Japanese people and drove
them into involvement with a World War. At the close of
the war, the state shrine was abolished with the stroke of
MacArthur's pen. But the myth was not abolished from
the hearts of the Japanese people. As Masao Takenaka
shows in his *Reconciliation and Renewal in Japan*, the
job of unmasking myths has to go on.

We have seen in our generation how National Socialism
brought the old Germanic tribal myths back on the
stage—a complete mythology with its own cult-objects,
its own dogma of National Purity, its own ethos, and its
own sacrifices of millions of young people to modern
Molochs. Tribal myths can be resurrected at any time.
There is no nation, no racial group in the entire world,
where some form of myth does not function. Many
national ideologies are, at close range, nothing but myths
in the garments of ideologies. The unmasking of myths is
a continuing task; we must keep our heads and stay
awake to them. Everywhere!

Along with racial myths we have race theories. Race
theories are myths rationalized. Race theorists try to give
the collective pride of particular racial groups a rational
and scientific basis. Luther once remarked that the mind
of man, the human reason, often acts the part of a
prostitute. It is always for sale and gladly puts itself at
the service of collective feelings and public opinion, of
pride, hate, and anger. Race theories are created when
theorists sell themselves to racial pride. Learned men
proclaim that one race is superior to another (particularly
in times of crisis or war) and that the hope of the nations
lies in the elimination of certain other races. Ruth Benedict calls race theories a form of superstition. She is right.
In the absence of a complete history of race theories, a
few remarks will have to suffice here. Just a few, so that
we may not forget.

The history of race theories really begins with the
Greeks, who in the judgment of many are the fathers of

theoretical thought. (This too is a myth of sorts, if one remembers the contributions of Asiatic culture. But, it is at least true that the Greeks played an exceptionally important role in the development of theoretical thinking.) Thales, one of the pre-Socratics, first thanks the fates that he was born a man and not an animal. Second, he thanks them that he was born a man and not a woman. And third, *that he was born a Greek and not a barbarian*. Even Plato and Aristotle reshaped racial myths into racial theories. They taught that certain peoples—in their case the Greeks—were called to rule over other men, while other peoples were called to subjection and slavery.

In 1907 Robert W. Shufeldt used his book *The Negro, A Menace to American Civilization* to saddle the Negro race with almost every conceivable disparaging stereotype. This monstrous diatribe is too shameful to relate. In Western Europe, Count Joseph Arthur de Gobineau (1816-1882) translated myth into theory to argue the superiority of the Aryan race, in particular the European, in his *Essay on the Inequality of the Human Races*. Richard Wagner's son-in-law, Houston Stewart Chamberlain, espoused the same idiocies in his *Foundations of the Nineteenth Century*. Both books were very popular in Germany and made an impact on Hitler and his colleagues.

Gobineau declared that the white race had a monopoly on everything beautiful, honest, trustworthy, and hospitable, as well as on intelligence and energy. Any mixing of races, he maintained, creates a generation of bastards who are either "attractive without vitality, or are vigorous without intelligence, or are intelligent and at the same time weak and lazy." This is the way theories of the superiority of the Nordic peoples and the inferiority of non-Nordics are generally put together.

With the help of such theories, Hitler argued that there was only one sacred human right, a right that entails a great responsibility, namely the right to keep the blood pure. Houston Chamberlain and his disciples had not hesitated to claim Jesus for the Nordic race after "proving" Him to have been of Teutonic origin. Every conceivable virtue was attributed to the Nordic race by these worshippers of Wodin: honesty, trustworthiness, sobriety, friendliness, hospitality, and so on and on and on. Hitler and his clique translated the theory into life, and so we came to know men who were "honest" like Goebbels, "sober" like Goering, "hospitable and friendly" like Himmler, and "trustworthy" like Hitler himself.

When Hitler had these theories published in such monstrous writings as Alfred Rosenberg's *Der Mythus des Zehnjahrhunderts (The Myth of the Twentieth Century),* the German scientific community raised no protests. The silence of the scientists has been laid out in a disturbingly factual brief by Karl Saller in his *Die Rassenlehre des National-Sozialismus in Wissenschaft und Propaganda (The Race Theory of National Socialism in Science and Propaganda)* (1961). We must also recall the theological scandal of many nominal Christians in Germany—though it must also be gratefully noted that some voices in the church did protest against the theory, the famous Barmen Declaration being the most fundamental rejection of racial theories ever formulated.

These days we are tempted to suppose that this sort of theory and the phoney materials used to build it have gone down the drain, and that vigilance against them is misdirected energy. But this is mistaken. The racial theories echoed in the Ossewabrandwag movement in South Africa at the time of World War II are obvious. What may not be so well known is that articles like the one from which I quote below have appeared as recently as 1969 in the church press. I quote Dr. M. W. Retief from his piece published in the *Kerkbode (Church Messenger)* of the Nederduits Gereformeerde Kerk, February 10, 1969:

> Do not think there is reason to accept the notion of the equality of all races; it is an idea that is propagated by

communism, international Jewry, and Americanism. The modern liberalism that exploits this notion was born in the emaciated and spiritually sick Europe of the post World War II period. The notion of the equality of all races is therefore an idea that trickled out of a sick Europe [i.e., post-Hitler Europe] and was taken over by international Jewry, to which a large section of the world press belong.

Statements like this are not unusual in South Africa. Apartheid—of which we will have more to say in a later chapter—is a practical expression given to the myth of the superiority of the white race and of the "natural rights" the white race has to subject other races to itself. Cecil Rhodes had a vision that was a first cousin to such myths, and Ian Smith is his modern-day prophet in Rhodesia.

Race theories are definitely not extinct, and they are not in the process of becoming extinct. Their power of survival derives from the fact that they are nourished from the deep, dark reservoir called racism. There are, to be sure, racial theories that argue the superiority of nonwhite races and that are colored reflections of white racial theories. There are Russian, Chinese, Ceylonese, African, and many other racial myths and theories. Concerning these, I need only remark that the nations who heard the biblical message early in their histories are most responsible and most guilty. Anyone who listens sympathetically to the Edda*, or whatever other myth, after having heard the Torah on the unity of the human race and the New Testament on the reunion of the human race through Jesus Christ surely burdens himself with enormous responsibility.

Finally, this remark. Everyone can share the raw materials for racial theories. The broad generalizations with which people of one race describe people of another race at any social gathering are the stuff from which race theories are concocted. This is why the unmasking of racial myths and racial theories is as imperative at the

*A 13th century collection of Nordic mythological verse.

cocktail party as it is in the university classroom and the church pulpit.

IMPERIALISM AND COLONIALISM

One of the phenomena that has long poisoned the relationships between races, and still poisons them, is aptly called imperialism. "Imperialism" is one of the clichés of modern history. It is knocked about in talk concerning many areas of modern life: political, historical, cultural, economic, and ideological. We want, first, to ask what imperialism actually is and what motives lie behind it. Then we want to try to see why this thing troubles relationships between races. And finally we want to talk about how the phenomenon of imperialism has to be evaluated in the light of God's promises and demands.

A. What Is Imperialism?

One way to begin getting at a thing is to analyze the word itself. The word "imperialism" is associated with the Latin *imperium, imperator, imperare*, etc. *Imperare* means to rule over someone or something. *Imperator* gets closer to imperialism. Now and then a Roman army officer got the commission to cross the boundaries of the Roman Empire (the Imperium) to annex new territory to the Imperium. When the officer returned with his troops, he was given the title *Imperator*. This called for a festive march into Rome, the monuments of which are still tourist attractions in Rome. The Imperator rode in a triumphal chariot at the head of the "imperial parade." Behind him marched the imperial troops, and after them were dragged representatives of the conquered tribes. These wore the garments of subjection. They carried objects from their own cultures to present to the Caesar as symbols of their subjection. All the while, the balconies rang out with "Ave Imperator, Ave Imperator." Today we understand imperialism as the striving of one state to use the people of another state as instruments for its purposes. Sometimes imperialism is expressed in brutal territorial expansion beyond natural or treaty-formed boundaries. When this occurs, imperialism takes the form of colonialism by conquest, penetration, subjection, or exploitation. But there are also forms of imperialism in which colonialism is absent but in which one people still uses another as the instrument of its own interests.

Imperialism is a universal phenomenon in history. Though Spanish and Portuguese imperialism, followed hard by the expansionism of the British, the Dutch, the Belgians, and the French, was the first example of modern imperialism, and though from the 16th until the end of the 19th centuries this Western imperialism was the most conspicuous form of it, imperialism is lodged deep in the tendencies of all nations. The history of the indigenous kingdoms of Asia and Africa in the pre-colonial period is rife with imperialism. And in more recent history, Japan and China, along with Russia, have also played an expansionistic role.

What motivations led nations toward imperialism? This question cannot be answered simply; the history of imperialism is far too complex for that. The imperialism of the Mongols (Ghenghis Khan) was based on motives different from those of the Greeks and the Romans. Nor has modern imperialism in the Western nations been driven by the same motives as drove the Caesars. Throughout history the reasons behind imperialism have differed according to time and place.

Still, it is possible to discover certain basic motives behind all imperialism. Sometimes all the motives converge. Sometimes we recognize only a few of them. The basic motives are (1) political-economic; (2) cultural; (3) nationalistic; (4) pseudo-religious; and (5) ideological.

(1) It hardly needs proof that *political-economic* motives figure large in imperialism. The mercantile imperialism of England, France, and the Netherlands arose in their efforts to take over the monopolies that the Spaniards and Portuguese had won in the treaty of Tordesillas of 1494. When the Peace of Utrecht was concluded at the close of the Wars of Spanish Succession, it was considered an enormous diplomatic victory—the partici-

pating power won the right of "asiento," which is to say, the right to carry on slave traffic in the Spanish colonies.

Imperialism always went hand in hand with annexation, protectorates, concessions, the creation of economic spheres of influence, the search for export markets with political side-purposes, the exploitation of cheap labor for export into the world markets, and so on. We are not making a judgment here. We only want to note the facts that anyone can see for himself in the history of imperialism. Mercantile imperialism spilled over into political imperialism. The protection of trade and production monopolies led to the development of political structures that bound the colonies to their motherlands.

(2) Another motive in imperialism has always been (and still is) *cultural*. The Greeks hoped to spread their culture through Asia Minor and Persia into the Indies. They wanted to hellenize the barbarians. The Romans sought to spread their Roman civilization and statecraft to all parts of the world. The cultural mission also played a large role in British imperialism. Cecil Rhodes discovered that whenever he extended British power with its "civilization" into Africa, he felt he was fulfilling a divine commission, as his letters so abundantly reveal. How much French imperialism was driven by a longing to benefit mankind with French culture is known to everyone. And when the United States took over the Philippines from the Spanish, Roosevelt spoke of it in terms of our "mission of civilization." Dutch imperialism too was in large measure motivated by cultural missionism.

(3) The *racial*, or *nationalistic*, motive has also deeply influenced imperialism from the beginning. The Greeks thought the Greek nation superior to all others. They called non-Greeks by the demeaning name *barbaroi*—that is, jabberers. They believed that their own national honor (recall the expeditions of Alexander the Great) obliged them to subject the "jabberers" to their superior Greek rule. The Romans too believed that their Roman-hood

gave them a duty to dominate other peoples. The Mongols in Central Asia were possessed of the same sense of obligation when they unleashed the Mongolian assaults in the direction of China and Bagdad. The British Empire, the Russian Empire, the Dutch Empire, the German Empire, the Nipponese Empire, etc. were all constrained by a burning desire to enhance the honor, the glory, and the power of their own nation. Sometimes a dynastic motive insinuated itself into the national (and racial) motive. The honor of certain dynasties had to be enhanced, as for example the honor of the Chinese imperial families, or the honor of Queen Victoria, the Japanese Mikado, or the Hohenzollern family.

(4) Another motive present in all phases of imperialism is the *pseudo-religious* motive. I call this motive pseudo-religious because anyone who uses the call to spread his religious convictions as a means to justify extending political power is abusing religion—certainly Christianity—at its core. The Lord Jesus commissioned His disciples to declare the Gospel to all creatures. The churches are called to carry on the task always and everywhere. But the Lord never gave His disciples a call to use the sword as an instrument of missions.

King Canute, who compelled the Danes to accept Christianity at the point of a sword; Charles the Great, who turned the Saxons into Christians with his sword; Peter of Amiens and the Popes, who used the name of Christ to organize the Crusades—all these men disfigured the image of Jesus Christ and crucified His Spirit anew, as Martin Luther said in his pamphlets against the Crusades. The same sort of thing is to be seen in Pope Nicholas V and Pope Alexander VI when they gave instructions to extend their political power into Asia, Africa, and the newly discovered American territories and at the same time to "spread the name of Jesus Christ." They proceeded from the false belief that the earthly sword had been given to the church. This same pseudo-religious motive played a role in the 16th and 17th centuries in the operations of the British and East India Company. Similarly with the Russian Orthodox and Greek Orthodox churches. Caesaropapism and Byzantianism have long been seedbeds of pseudo-religious imperialism. When Moscow took over the role once filled by Byzantium after the fall of Constantinople, it assumed the same pseudo-religious pose, taking over as the Third Rome and clothing itself in the mantle of religious ideals.

Islam too employed religion in the service of Moslems' imperialistic expansion. The establishment of a Moslem Commonwealth during the first four caliphs and during the rule of the Omayyads (7th-10th centuries) was driven by the conviction that the Moslem generals carried a mandate to expand the dominion of the Kingdom of Allah as widely as possible. It would not be hard to show that other non-Western forms of imperialism used still other religions in this pseudo-religious way, especially Buddhism.

(5) The present century is the age of ideology and of the collision of ideologies. The *ideological* motive is strong in the most modern forms of imperialism. Moscow, Peking, and Havana, the Communist radiation centers, all justify their efforts to expand the political-economic power of Communism by their conviction that they are models of salvation and the panacea for all ills. The tendency to propagate the American way of life as *the* life style for all and to make the world safe for American-style democracy has loaned a quasi-religious tone to American diplomacy since the time of John Foster Dulles. In world Communism the purity of the ideological motive is diluted in the hearts of many who still pay lip service to it. And the American ideology has worn a bit threadbare against the background of the internal American situation. But it is still undeniable that in post-colonial imperialism, the ideological motive has played its role in new forms and with new slogans, and it is likely to go on doing so.

B. An Evaluation of Imperialism

What have been the consequences of imperialism?

In the area of *economics*, imperialism has accomplished a great deal through the discovery and development of the economic potential of the dominated lands. No one should try to deny this. Entire areas which had been closed to world business were opened wide. Territories where economic possibilities went untouched were exploited. But one thing characteristic of every form of imperialist and colonialist economy was this—the economic interests of the colonizers were given top priority and the economic interests of the colonized peoples were given second-rating at best and much lower priority at worst. The "economic drainage policy" was typical of every imperialist economy. The largest part of the profits was siphoned off to the investors of capital. No balance was sought between the interests of the colonized land and the interests of the capitalists. The result, socially, was that respect for and rewards to the labor of the colonists were extremely low.

Culturally, imperialism has made unquestioned contributions to the development of the lesser-developed areas. But the cultural interests of the colonizers were again given priority. Education and the sciences were stressed only in so far as they were needed to further the imperialist interests of the dominating powers.

The *social-psychological* results of imperialism are grimly depressing. Every form of imperialism has nourished characteristics in both the domineering and the dominated that have poisoned genuine human relationships. The dominators have nourished a luxurious sense of superiority in their bosoms, a feeling that Kraemer once referred to as the "persistent self-nomination to leadership." It was a sense of superiority that ruined morale because it was based only on power and not on actual character.

Imperialism also fostered an inability and an unwillingness to get inside the life and hopes of the peoples among whom the imperialists lived and worked. Their inability or unwillingness to understand them was the seedbed of superficial and uninformed generalizations about the peoples they controlled.

Imperialism, on the other side, breeds among the dominated people feelings of rage toward their masters, feelings of mistrust and offense, and a sense of inferiority that has prevented a genuine meeting of human beings, heart to heart.

Ethically, imperialism has managed in certain instances to convince subjected people to put away some admittedly bad practices (e.g., the burning of widows in India and ritualistic murder in other places). But against this must be set the fact that imperialism has never hesitated to use such unethical means as deception, bribery, theft, and war when they were necessary to advance the imperialist's interests.

The history of imperialism is full of beautiful promises during times of crises followed by ruthless promise-breaking when times were normal again. When Lawrence of Arabia threw down his colonel's insignia before the Cabinet in London after the First World War, he meant it as a dramatic protest against the fact that he was forced after the war to take back almost all the promises he had made to Arabian states in the name of the British crown. But promise-breaking was typical of all imperialist countries. It is of the essence of imperialism, and will always be as long as imperialism lives.

Testing imperialism by God's standards, the standards of the Sermon on the Mount and the summary of the Law of God, we are forced to only one conclusion —imperialism has poisoned brotherhood between the races, corrupted international associations, set might above right, and divided and conquered rather than heal and serve.

Yet we must acknowledge that this is not the whole story of imperialism. In his magnificent speech on "Im-

perialism and National Self-Expression," given at the first
world student missionary conference in Basel, 1935, Hendrik Kraemer delivered a crushing indictment of Western
imperialism, but he also showed how the West, throughout its imperialist phase, was troubled by the very Christian conscience and moral ideals that it pretended to be
the bearer of. Under the influence of such varied figures
as Monroe, Burke, and Van Deventer, who laid the
groundwork for a more moral view of politics and who
remodelled the system of conquest, penetration, and
domination into a paternalistic "politics of emancipation," and under the influence too of growing self-doubts
in the West, a trend was started toward political, cultural,
and economic self-expression within the colonies, a trend
that led to the decline of colonialism as the prevailing
system. In this phase of the "politics of emancipation"
and increasing national self-expression, Christian missions
performed an important prophetic and priestly function.

Imperialism came to be ministered unto. But in the last
stages of its history, it showed signs of the spirit of Him
who came not to be ministered unto but to minister.
Stephen Neill has told this side of the story in his book
Colonialism and Christian Mission (1966), as Max Warren
has done in his *Social History and Christian Mission*
(1967). But Warren probed most deeply in his remarkable
book *Caesar, the Beloved Enemy.* In a chapter called
"Theology of Imperialism," he warned against a one-
sided judgment of imperialism. Now I do not agree with
Warren's thesis; I think that imperialism has most often
been credited with too much. But Warren does open our
eyes to the fact that history was not written only by
imperialist potentates, generals, robbers, empire-builders,
and the like, but that God was writing His own history,
crisscrossing through the history of men. The same Bible
that exposes the sins of the Roman Empire shows us,
without embarrassment, that God used the language, the
laws, the manners, the culture of the Roman Empire to
further the interests of the Gospel of Jesus Christ in the

"fulness of time." Looking at history from the perspective of the biblical vision, every honest investigator has to agree that the history of imperialism was *not* from top to bottom a history of sin and unrighteousness.

In this connection, we may mention the remarkable book written by the Indian historian K. M. Panikkar, *Asia and Western Dominance*. It is one of the sharpest anti-colonial and anti-imperialist documents I know of. But even Panikkar concedes that Western imperialism left some good aftereffects in Asia and Africa, effects that Asia and Africa will never abandon. He mentions among other things that the former colonial territories received a vast body of legislation, a system of laws that, while not infallible, laid the basis for further legislative development. Loosely jointed areas have been integrated as nations as local despots were overthrown. Large cities have developed in Asia and Africa. Great areas have been brought together as single political and cultural entities. The isolation of Asia and Africa was set forever behind them.

The same acknowledgments were evident at the Afro-Asian Conference in Bandung in 1955. Richard Wright has given us an account of it in his book *The Color Curtain*. He wrote of the "Western World in Bandung" to illustrate the depth of Western influence in the ideals of the conference. The conference was created by those who had been reviled, insulted, and injured by the sins of Western imperialism. And yet it was a conference of those whose encounter with the West led them to dream, to foster ideals, and to draw the blueprints of a new future. Carlos Romulo, who bitterly inveighed against the racism of the West, was also the man who, along with Nehru, recalled to the delegates how "this white world, though possessed by racism, also managed to achieve many other things. Just as Western political thought has given us the basis for our concepts of political freedom, justice, and equality, so it was Western science that demolished the mythology of race in this generation."

But whatever the benefits that have come from imperialism, we must never fail to emphasize that people have
got to unlearn the habit of exploiting one another, dominating each other, and using one another as means and
instruments. Nations have to learn anew to serve one
another, to help and support each other. This is why we
are called to fight against imperialism in any form and
from whatever direction it comes and in whatever cloak it
disguises itself. The struggle is not over by a long shot, for
the spirit of imperialism is still alive.

C. The Continuing Struggle Against Imperialism in Our Time

The spirit of imperialism is not dead. It is very much
alive and wears many faces, some old and some new.

1. THE STRUGGLE AGAINST OLD-STYLE IMPERIALISM

Portuguese colonialism in Angola, Mozambique, and
Guinea is an example of old-style imperialism. The complete history of this phase of imperialism is still to be
written, in spite of the publicity it has had in recent
years. My purpose here will be served, I think, by recall-
ing the story of Eduardo Mondlane, the former head of
the liberation front in Mozambique. Mondlane was murdered in a bombing attack early in 1969. Like Bonhoeffer, who had abandoned a place of safety abroad to join
the struggle against Hitler, Mondlane, a doctor of philos-
ophy, a Harvard graduate, and for five years a member
of the Security Council of the United Nations, gave up
the comfort and safety of a public and academic post
with the United Nations to go back to his homeland to
lead the struggle against colonial tyranny, a conflict in
which he contributed an unusual combination of political
realism and moral integrity. A friend wrote at the time of
his death: "In danger every day, he was never afraid.
Living always in the center of racial conflicts, he was too
big for feelings of hostility." In the midst of tragic chaos,

this Presbyterian sociologist kept alive a vision of hope, of faith, and of love. He was murdered, like Martin Luther King, at a moment when his leadership was most acutely needed. His widow, Janet Mondlane, kept up the work the Mozambique Institute had begun, to promote education in those areas where the yoke of colonialism had been thrown off.

It is not for me to pronounce judgment on the means and methods used by Mondlane in his struggle against colonialism in Mozambique. But I must point out that we, from afar, are not permitted to take a balcony seat from which to watch the struggle. The International Conference of Solidarity, held in Khartum, the Sudan, in January of 1969, demonstrated how seriously the Communist world movement is attempting to manipulate the six liberation movements in East and South Africa for its own ends. We see the very same thing happening as happened when French and Dutch colonialism was liquidated, when the West showed no understanding as Moscow tried to manipulate the national liberation fighters. It is our job to let Portugal know where we stand, it is our job to give places like the Mozambique Institute our support with words and acts, it is our job to do everything possible to bring the representatives of Portugal and the national liberationists to the conference table in order to resolve their conflicts and to work for the liquidation of the colonial structure and the building of new relationships.

2. THE STRUGGLE AGAINST SEMI-COLONIALISM IN LATIN AMERICA

The tension-laden developments in Latin America demand our close attention. Cuba, Chile, Peru, Colombia, Brazil, Haiti are in the news of the world as never before. In the 19th century, the Latin-American lands obtained their political emancipation under the leadership of figures like Simon Bolivar, but they are still looking for their social and economic independence. Economically, the Latin-American countries exist in a semi-colonial status.

André Siegfried demonstrated this already in 1934 in his book *Latin America*. In this masterful analysis of the concept of colonialism, he points out that colonial status is not simply to be equated with political dependence. Colonialism is first of all an economic reality. Whenever the larger portion of the economic affairs of a country is in the hands of foreigners, is stimulated and managed by outside interests, you have a country that exists in a semi-colonial status. A colonial area is, in the first place, a country that lives in economic servitude.

Several Latin-American countries have become acutely aware of their economic colonial status. The reaction to Nelson Rockefeller's trip in June of 1969 was a symptom of this awareness. The weakness of President Kennedy's *Alliance of Progress,* begun in 1961, was not that it set loose a stream of American capital toward Latin America, nor that North Americans were encouraged to take up residence there to bring their know-how to the lands south of the border, but that these actions were not tied to conditions that would result in the throwing off of Latin America's semi-colonial status and contribute to the building of a genuine Latin-American social-economic order. It is absolutely essential that any help we give to the Latin-American countries function to build a genuinely national and regional social-economic order, including the aspects of wages, prices, and management.

3. SEMI-COLONIALISM IN EAST EUROPE AND EAST ASIA

Lenin wrote his famous work *Imperialism: the Latest Stage in the Development of Capitalism* in 1917. Since then Russian Communism has been trumpeted as the greatest anti-imperialistic force in the modern world. It may be true that Russian Communism has, for many

reasons, stimulated the movement against colonialism in
Asia and Africa and in that respect has hastened the
process of decolonization. But the anti-imperialist slogans
of Russian Communism should not blind us to the fact
that Russia's own relationships with its satellites in East
Europe have been brutally imperialist in design and method. Without doubt, these relations have gone hand in
hand with a collective security system designed as a front
against the specter of a West Germany drunk on nationalism again. Still, it is undeniable that the Russian-East
European relationships are shaped by the same lust for
domination and exploitation that Lenin skewered
Western imperialism with. Mercantile considerations,
forced trade and labor markets, the exploitation of East
European countries for Russian interests, the maintenance of spheres of influence through governments foisted
on the people from the outside—everything that we can
remember as typical of Western colonialism in the old
days is now as visible as daylight in Russia's relations with
its East European satellites. Anti-imperialism cannot be
judged by slogans. The Brezhnev doctrine that was used
to frustrate the hopes of the younger generation in
Czechoslovakia is as imperialistic as any instance of "em-
pire-building" in the old days of out-and-out colonialism.

The same may be said of China. The tension between
China and Russia is really a conflict between two imperialist powers, each straining at the leash to protect its
sphere of influence, just as the Western colonial powers
did in their confrontations with each other in the 19th
century. And the position of China vis-à-vis Tibet and
Taiwan is every bit as imperialistic as all the classic forms
of imperialism. One sees posters everywhere in Peking
heralding China as the standard-bearer for all the colored
peoples of the world in their fight against imperialism. It
may well be that the developing areas of the world can
learn a good deal from China, but the lessons would be
more digestible if the teachers were willing to grant the

same kind of freedom from imperialist influences that China has rightly demanded for itself.

RACE RELATIONS WITHIN THE NEWER COUNTRIES

But racial injustice and exploitation exists not only on the intercontinental and international level. Equally urgent is the need for harmony between the various racial groups or subgroups *within* many countries. We cannot attempt a large survey of these tensions, for to do so would require a book by itself. A few observations will make the point.

We all followed, aghast, the terrible story of the civil war between the federal government of Nigeria and the Ibos in Biafra. We may recall that when Nigeria began its existence as an independent state, it was represented to the world as the most harmonious decolonization effort of this century, accompanied by the best will among all for inter-tribal cooperation. That image was shattered in unspeakable pain.

In the Sudan, Arabs from up North have collided for centuries with blacks from down South. In Burma, we still find Buddhists engaged in bloody confrontation with tribes from the North. In all of South-East Asia, tensions between the Polynesians and the Chinese are rife, as is seen in Malaya and Indonesia today. But Western lands have had their taste of such tensions too. Consider the Hungarians in East Europe, the Walloons and Flemish in Belgium, the Welsh in Great Britain, the Bretons in France, the Indians in the U.S., and the Eskimos in Canada.

This aspect of racial tension was included in the discussions of race relationships in general at the assembly of the World Council of Churches in Uppsala. After the First World War, the Wilson Doctrine of the "self-determination of nations" was frequently drawn on by the various ecumenical organs; but the council at Uppsala handled this doctrine a bit more carefully. Rightly so. Anyone who pushes self-determination too glibly will soon discover that Africa is split up into countless minuscule political fragments which are incapable of independent existence economically, socially, or politically. The same is true in Asia. Throwing such slogans around as "Free Ambon" or "Free Papoea" is very easy but very often ignores hard reality.

In Uppsala, it seems to me, some very wise words were spoken on this subject. The declaration concerning minorities and majorities inside nations went this way: All peoples have the right of self-determination. This is a basic requisite of human dignity and of a genuine family of nations. But nations are seldom made up of a wholly homogenous people. Most nations contain racial, cultural, or religious minorities. These minorities have the right to choose their own life style in so far as their choice does not deprive other groups of the same choice. Majorities can be insensitive and tyrannical, with the result that minorities need protection. This is a special responsibility of the church of Him who is the champion of the oppressed. But if the rights of the minorities are pushed too far, they may threaten the justice and stability of the existence of the nations. That a majority should be held down by a minority is just as irreconcilable with justice as is persecution of a minority by a majority.

There is no uniform and satisfactory solution to these tensions. Nations usually have to be satisfied with compromise solutions. None of them is practicable in all circumstances and none offers a guarantee of peace. Tensions must be accepted and creatively used; but the churches must be prepared to present at least some criteria of human value as a standard. Majorities must understand that they have responsibilities for granting the greatest possible freedom to their minorities, and the minorities must recognize that majorities too have rights.

The churches must defend the minorities whenever they are oppressed or threatened. Sometimes minorities must be cautioned to moderate their struggles for their ideals. But the church must help the majorities to find creative ways of responding to the impatience of the minorities in their struggle for justice.

This balanced declaration is worth the world's attention. In regard to Indonesia, for example, some people in the World Council foster the rights of the Indonesians of Chinese descent, while others support the rights of the population of West Irian. Meanwhile, West Europeans ought to be helping the central Indonesian government to respond creatively to the impatience of all the groups who experience a sense of frustration and unfairness. The English have the same task in Nigeria, and we are grateful to note that several are working at it, sometimes contrary to public opinion. The All Africa Conference of Churches has the same task in the Sudan, and the East Asia Christian Conference has it in Ceylon and Vietnam.

We have seen how minorities can be liquidated, trapped, and down-trodden. But things do not have to go that way. Things can and must change. In pain and anguish, racial groups can often learn to accept one another and to live in justice with one another. Let us strengthen the hands of those who want to steer in that direction.

This chapter has been an effort to see the broad strokes of the struggle against racial injustice and of the struggle for better race relations. Before observing spots in the world where the struggle for justice is most pressing at this time, we will devote a chapter to the churches and their place in the struggle at the present time.

Chapter Four

The Churches in the
Struggle for Racial Justice

THE ECUMENICAL MOVEMENT
AND RACIAL JUSTICE

Jesus' mandate in His world-embracing missionary commission demands not only that we baptize people from all nations, but also that we teach them and live before them in obedience to all that He has commanded us, including the bearing of His teaching on race relations (Matt. 28:16-29). Now without doubt the churches in all parts of the world have exercised an incalculable influence on race relations simply through their proclamation of God's promises and demands in this sphere. But it must also be said that history throws up too many situations in which the churches have sabotaged this message, have bargained God's promises away for a racist ideology. We will not have a chance within the limits of this book to portray much of the glory and misery of the churches' achievements and failures. Father Yves Congar, O.P., wrote a most remarkable book called *The Catholic Church and the Race Question*, published as part of the UNESCO series. And in that same series W. A. Visser 't Hooft gave us a lucid and well-documented study on *The Ecumenical Movement and the Race Problem* (Paris,

1954), in which he offers a bird's-eye view of the part the World Council of Churches has played in both regional and international situations. Both of these excellent studies lay their emphasis on the problem of anti-semitism.

The most grotesque explosion of anti-semitism of all time still reverberated powerfully through the years when these books were written, and it was natural for these authors to stress that dimension of race relations. If I somewhat ignore the problem of anti-semitism as it comes to light in these books, it is not because I am unaware that this horrible reality is still alive in the world. It does exist. The symptoms of it are showing in many places—in Poland, in Russia, and in West Germany, not to forget North America. It also appears in the Mideast among those intoxicated with the fantasy of destroying the state of Israel. But our concern is particularly with the racial dimensions of the relationship between the rich and the impoverished countries.

For this purpose we should point to another book that appeared in 1969, called *The Grey Book*. It was written by J. M. Snoek, who until recently worked in Tiberias (Israel), and offers us material that complements the works of Congar and Visser 't Hooft. I would like to update this material to cover more recent history by using contributions of the general assembly of the World Council in Uppsala and, from a bit later on, the consultation on racism held in Notting Hill, London, in May of 1969.

UPPSALA AND THE STRUGGLE AGAINST RACISM

A. The Sense of Urgency at Uppsala

The statements, reports, and involvements of the International Missionary Council and later the World Council of Churches in the area of race relations would make a considerable library. The material is all filed in Geneva and is available for anyone to read. Those who do read it will be impressed. But the sense of urgency was never felt so keenly as it was in the general assembly meetings at Uppsala in 1968. The brief close-ups provided by various documentary films offered delegates a chance to see specific instances of white racism and left every viewer with a summons to recognize his own responsibility and obligation.

Two addresses in the plenary evening session brought this even closer to the participants. James Baldwin made the deepest impression. He bore the stigmata of the injuries that men inflict on human values—they were in his eyes, in his style of speech, in his volcanic verbal eruptions, and in his intense gestures. This son of a Baptist preacher, this one-time minister who deserted official Christendom, seemed to feel more radically than anyone how the Son of Man is betrayed by racism. His words grasped the audience unforgettably: "There are areas in the world where Christianity has the power to change the structures—if it will."

Baldwin was followed by Lord Caradon, British delegate to the United Nations and a man whose profound identification with Africa (it was he who, with the Bantu teacher Matthews, drew up the emergency program for the African churches) and with the problems of decolonization gave him special qualifications to speak. His propositions may have been a bit romantic (a new worldwide youth movement against racism), but what moved him was his intense fear that the association of nations would continue to roll on toward a racial war unless the centrifugal forces driving peoples apart were countered by the centripetal forces in Christ.

B. The Statements on Racism

The questions involving race relations were handled under the section devoted to "international justice and peace." I will now quote the part of the report that bears on racism.

Contemporary racism robs all human rights of their meaning, and is an imminent danger to world peace. The crucial nature of the present situation is emphasized by the official policies of certain governments, racial violence in many countries, and the racial component in the gap between rich and poor nations. Only immediate action directed to root causes can avoid widespread violence or war.

Racism is a blatant denial of the Christian faith. (1) It denies the effectiveness of the reconciling work of Jesus Christ, through whose love all human diversities lose their divisive significance; (2) it denies our common humanity in creation and our belief that all men are made in God's image; (3) it falsely asserts that we find our significance in terms of racial identity rather than in Jesus Christ.

Racism is linked with economic and political exploitation. The churches must be actively concerned for the economic and political well-being of exploited groups so that their statements and actions may be relevant. In order that victims of racism may regain a sense of their own worth and be enabled to determine their own future, the churches must make economic and educational resources available to underprivileged groups for their development to full participation in the social and economic life of their communities. They should also withdraw investments from institutions that perpetuate racism. They must also urge that similar assistance be given from both the public and private sectors. Such economic help is an essential compensatory measure to counteract and overcome the present systematic exclusion of victims of racism from the main stream of economic life. The churches must also work for the change of those political processes which prevent the victims of racism from participating fully in the civic and governmental structures of their countries.

Racism employs fallacious generalizations and distortions to sustain its existence, and these result in personal denigration, segregation and other forms of isolation. The churches must eradicate all forms of racism from their own life. That

many have not done so, particularly where institutional
racism assumes subtle forms, is a scandal. The churches
must also fight to secure legislation to eliminate racism.
This will involve new approaches in education and the mass
media, so that false value-judgments can be eliminated and
the true grounds of human dignity made evident to all
mankind.

Racism produces counter-racism as a defensive measure
for human survival. It also perpetuates itself from generation to generation. The Church must break this vicious
spiral. It must confront individuals who hold racial prejudices with the truth about our common humanity and
emphasize the personal worth of all men. It must demonstrate that the grace of God is sufficient to reconcile and
unite all members of the human race.

This is the portion of the official report that was sent
to the member churches for "study and action." The
statement on the struggle against racism is rightly set
within the framework of the struggle for fundamental
human rights. It was Robert K. A. Gardiner, executive
secretary of the Economic Commission for Africa (U.N.),
who put his finger on this equation. Men like Albert
Luthuli and Martin Luther King, Jr., he insisted, were
primarily crusaders for *human* rights. Gardiner pointed
out the frustrations that occur whenever contacts are
made between different cultures, frustrations that often
get in the way of and poison human relations; in this
regard he showed how racial tensions flare up not only
between whites and blacks but between Africans and
Asians (in Africa) and between racial subgroups within
the larger racial groups. Everything he said was burdened
by a concern for potential explosions of violence that are
ripe for happening in many places.

As I listened to the discussions and read the reports, I
recalled the first Christian World Youth Conference in
1939, just before the war broke out. The threat of war
hung heavy over every session. In Uppsala, the threat of

racial tensions shadowed us. One of the black leaders said to me: "Today, victims of racism, beaten and embittered, are still ready to talk. I fear that tomorrow we will see them closed-mouthed and bitter, determined to fight their way through the problems." What, then, can we do?

Lord Caradon was unrealistic and romantic when he called for a "crusade of youth" for racial justice. But it is absolutely necessary to launch an assault on the self-satisfaction and smugness that slacken the struggle for racial justice everywhere, an assault that must shake them to their roots. And Lord Caradon saw correctly that the younger generation around the world is not going to be fooled with clichés and perpetual postponements.

Uppsala needed a follow-up. How hard this would be became clear during the times when, in the smaller committee meetings, North Nigerians and Biafrans, white and black Americans, delegates from the nations in conflict in the Mideast, met each other in long, difficult, and apparently fruitless discussion. But Uppsala was not the place to carry meetings like these through. This has to be done in regional meetings. There was a time when the churches thought they had done their jobs when the reports were published, recommendations made, and declarations broadcast. The World Council was of this mind once. But that time is gone. Church fellowships have not finished their task when reports are voted on in the august assemblies. This is finally becoming clear to us. The churches also have the job of stimulating movement that will actually effect changes in specific structures.

THE NOTTING HILL CONSULTATION

Part of the homework that Uppsala assigned was begun with the consultation on racism held in Notting Hill, London, May 19-24, 1969. Within the structure of the World Council, a consultation has the job of going into specific problems by means of dialogue with people who are directly involved and, having gotten intimately in-

formed, to make recommendations to the Council itself.
A consultation does not speak or act in the name of the
Council; it only advises the Council.

Several things about this consultation are worth
noting. In the first place, as one reads the documents
from this consultation, he is struck by the honest effort
to provide complete information about the symptoms of
white racism and black and brown counter-racism as they
appear not only in individual behavior but in the social
structures and power structures in which racism is invested. In the second place, the consultation not only
talked about racial revolution or "black power" but involved people in direct talk with representatives of these
movements. Mr. Oliver Tambo, successor to Albert Luthuli as chairman of the African National Congress
(which is outlawed in South Africa), spoke with no
restrictions. And Roy Sawh, leader of the Black Power
group in England, was fully involved in the consultation,
so much so that his presence required frequent alterations
in the agenda. In spite of their radical criticism of the
church, this militant group, which has broken off com-
munications with most segments of white society, is still
willing to talk to the churches because they have not
given up hope that the churches are still honestly concerned to support the struggle for racial justice.

The words of the black militants sent a shock through
delegates of the Western churches. But amid the tumult
of human voices it seemed as though the voice of the
living God came through here and there, in a new way,
like the old way of the prophets, when the "foundations
of the thresholds shook at the voice of him who
called . . ." (Isa. 6:4). A longing look over, one of the
delegates wrote later, for a translation of the Word of
God so powerful that it would in fact change the situation in the world. Some hint of hope, maybe induced by
memories of the word of Jeremiah: "I will cleanse them
from all the guilt of their sin against me, and I will forgive
all the guilt of the sin and rebellion against me. And this

city shall be to me a name of joy, a praise and a glory before all the nations of the earth who hear of all the good that I do for them . . ." (Jer. 33:8,9).

A third impression one has of the consultation is of a genuine wrestling for a theological diagnosis of the racial conflicts in our world. The contributions by Robert Nelson stimulated a hard try at bringing theological insights to bear on the sociological data, to pierce through sociological analyses into the human reservoirs of racial sin and to the necessity of authentic conversion and reconciliation.

Finally, we should mention the search for concrete action against the evils of racial injustice. At first there was talk of reparation so that at least some surface effects of racial sins might be undone by repaying something of what those sins had taken away from the colored peoples. This suggestion was put down from all sides as being hasty, ill-considered, foolish, utopian, and the like. But is it not a fact that confessing guilt for racial injustice must lead to concrete gestures toward undoing the results of that sin, to a will to create a social and economic balance between white and black peoples? If we say that the proposals made at Notting Hill, and the "black manifesto" proclaimed from a few white pulpits in the U.S., are impractical, we are obligated to make an all-out search, in company with the victims of racism, for alternative actions.

Here are a few statements taken from the Notting Hill declaration:

> (1) Wherever the churches identify themselves with the status quo, they form part of the race problem instead of being an agent of healing.
>
> (2) If the churches indeed want to be relevant in this critical time, they cannot rest with individual acts, but must act as a community. The churches must, further, be instruments of justice, and not of love alone. In our institutionalized world, justice is the most profound manifestation of love.

(3) The consultation recommends to the member
churches of the World Council that they endorse the principle of reparation, to the end that a more favorable balance
of economic power may be promoted.

The events at Notting Hill provoked some head-shaking
here and there. But whatever one may think about this
consultation, he will have to admit that the Christian
community can no longer think it has done enough when
it has published some declarations, that it has the calling
to stimulate change, and that one way to get change
started is to translate information, study, and declarations into action and experimentation. The question left
after Notting Hill was how the Central Committee of the
World Council would respond to its resolutions.

THE CENTRAL COMMITTEE AND NOTTING HILL

The Central Committee met in Canterbury from August 12 through August 23, 1969. Its task was to define
its position with respect to the resolutions and recommendations made at Notting Hill. We will limit our survey
to the most important considerations and proposals the
committee set before the member churches. The document issued by the Central Committee recognized that
the urgency of the struggle against racism demands of the
churches a deeper understanding, new approaches, and
reconciling acts, acts that may be very costly.

The concept of reparation, according to the document,
could not be ignored, now that it had been put on the
agenda during the consultations at Notting Hill. Many of
the churches that had been confronted with the demand
for reparations belonged to the ecumenical fellowship
and were faced with the need to give a meaningful response. Yet, the committee continued, the concept of
reparation is inadequate, because its attempt to overturn
the guilt of the past is simplistic, because its demand for

financial repayment tends to ignore the need for compassion, brotherhood, and fellowship. The Gospel, after all, speaks to us about the price of reconciliation, a price demanded of those who have suffered as well as of those who have caused the suffering. The churches must therefore move beyond benevolence, offerings, and traditional programs toward relevant and sacrificial actions that can lead to new relations, to a recognition of the worth and rights of all men, to a radical reconstruction of our social life. If justice is to be achieved in our world, there must be a redistribution of economic resources to support a redistribution of political power and to make cultural self-determination meaningful. The moral leadership of the churches can be demonstrated in a transfer of resources as a shared act of the ecumenical fellowship. This is the gist of the Central Committee's answer to Notting Hill.

The committee's document is accompanied by a five-year plan for the World Council's role in the struggle against racism. This plan emphasizes regional activities, regional research, regional consultations, and regional actions. All churches are urged to devote themselves with a new vigor to the problem of race relations, to the education and conversion of church members by providing study materials for them including theological treatments of the race question.

The committee voted to designate funds for the five-year plan. Beyond this, however, it also decided to provide the sum of $200,000, taken from the reserve fund of the World Council, as a special fund to support organizations whose goal is to aid victims of racial injustice, whenever the purposes of the organization involved agree with the general purposes of the World Council. The fund's purpose is to support the struggle for economic, social, and political justice. Further, member churches were asked to contribute, by way of special offerings, another $300,000.

The document ends with these words:

> Our fight is not against flesh and blood, but against the
> powers of evil, against the deeply-entrenched demonic
> forces of racial prejudice and hate. We are called to exorcise
> these devils. They work through social, economic, and
> political structures, but the root of the problem still lies in
> human sin. And only God's love and man's response to it
> can eradicate these sins. The World Council's program is
> only a part of that answer. God's love and not man's hate
> will finally overcome. By the love of God, in the power of
> His Spirit, "we shall overcome some day."

The World Council has been involved with the racial
question since its origin. But it never before addressed the
problem so concretely as it has since Uppsala and Notting
Hill. But this is at the top levels of organization. What has
to happen now is for the Christian communities to act in
their local areas in response to the appeal, and to walk
the hard way clearly marked on the map for the Christian
journey.

LOCAL AND REGIONAL CHURCHES
IN THE RACIAL QUESTION

While it undeniably lies within the scope of the worldwide church organizations to minister in their way to
reconciliation between the races, it is also obvious that
the local and regional churches live where the issues really
come to the cutting edge. The early churches, both regionally and locally, were interracial. The congregations
at Jerusalem, Antioch, Ephesus, Philippi, and the like,
were never limited to a single race. This was true of the
church throughout the first several centuries. One of the
most remarkable aspects of the life of the earliest Christian communities was just this, that Christians demonstrated they could embrace one another in their congregations with a grace-inspired indifference to race. The edict
of the Roman emperor Galerius, in fact, makes a point of

saying that Christians proved to have the power to bring the races together. The emperor, of course, thought this was nonsense, and dangerous besides; but he did find it noteworthy enough to make a point of it. Hermas declared that Christians had received, as a gift of grace from the Lord, the ability to unite people of various races. He writes: "The stones of the church are gathered from several hills and at the start are of many kinds, but as they are hewn and brought together in one building, they fit together in harmony" (*Similitudo* 9:4 and 9:17).

The episcopal dioceses of Alexandria, Carthage, and Hippo were definitely interracial. Augustine's diocese (Augustine himself being of mixed blood) included African as well as Roman members, and this in spite of the fall of the Roman Empire, in spite of the Vandals, and in spite of the Donatist schism. When new churches arose as a result of Western missions, the members were almost always interracial at the beginning (even in Cape Town, South Africa). It took time to turn the churches into ethnically divided memberships.

In a striking chapter of his study of the ecumenical movement's relation to the race question, Visser 't Hooft asks the question, "Can Ethnic Churches Be Justified?" We find churches all over Asia and Africa which, while they are not strictly limited to single tribes, are pretty much defined by tribal affiliations in their sociological structures. Indonesia, for example, has its Batak, its Javanese, its Moluccan, and its Minahassan churches. There is the Tiv church in Nigeria, the Bantu in South Africa. There are several tribal churches in Kenya. Can the perpetuation of this sort of more or less ethnically defined church be justified? Visser 't Hooft answers this question with two theses:

(1) The existence of separate churches on this basis cannot be justified theologically. But the existence of this sort of church can, under some circumstances, be justified on pastoral grounds.

(2) The formation of separate ethnic churches can be

seen only as a very temporary solution to the problems of
race and nation within the church. The clear purpose
must be to achieve a supra-ethnic, or supra-racial church
as soon as is feasible. In this matter, the sociological
structure of the church's environment can definitely not
be a decisive reason for not proceeding toward a supra-
racial church fellowship; for the church's calling is to
show the way to unrestricted brotherhood between men
and women of all nations and peoples.

With Visser 't Hooft's basic position I am in whole-
hearted agreement. But I do think that his theses are a bit
overstated in details. In the first place, there may also
have been missionary explanations for the formation of
ethnic churches at the beginning of this century. How so?
Well, it seems undeniable that a particular tribe or group
of generically associated tribes could be most easily
reached by a church that is made up of members of that
same tribe, and who used the language of that tribe, and
who understood its cultural patterns. This makes it un-
derstandable that the Western missionaries who were the
teachers of the new churches actually fostered tribal
churches. They have pointed out, however, that it is
actually better to speak, for example, of the Church of
Christ in Batakland than to speak of the Batak Church,
for this makes it clear that anyone who happens to live in
a given area has a place within the church of that area,
regardless of his tribal background. And in practice, local
or more or less ethnically defined churches never exist
exclusively of one tribe, but of several tribes.

Sociological factors can also be reasons for accepting
the formation of temporary ethnic churches. In Asia and
Africa it is highly important for contact to continue
between village or bush congregations and the city
churches. Exodus goes on constantly from village to
town. But experience shows that the urban communities
in Asia and Africa are not formed as a melting pot; they
are made up of several enclaves attached together, each
enclave made up of people from a single area. Churches

arise within the separate enclaves in the city, and they function as a kind of home away from home, a reception center and a recreation center of fellowship for people fresh from the bush, or village. This sort of situation is not odd, and anyone who can imagine himself in a strange city away from his village for the first time can appreciate the value of such a fellowship refuge.

Still, I completely agree with Visser 't Hooft's view that one of the central purposes of the church is to bring out into the open the unity of the races in Jesus Christ. This goal is in fact being worked at in many ways. In the first place, it is part of the cooperation between various ethnically defined churches within federations of churches, such as are coming into existence in Asia and Africa. In the second place, it is coming to pass in occasional fusions between churches. An example of this is the Church of South India. Thirdly, experiments are going on in many cities with the building of interracial congregations. I have been in close touch with one church in Jakarta for some twenty years now in which members of thirteen different ethnic groups have learned to live and work together. And in Durban, South Africa, there is a *deur mekaar kerk* (mixed church) in which people from several ethnic origins live together. Interracial experiments like these are highly needed if only to emphasize that ethnically defined churches should not remain permanently so and to serve as anticipations of what is really intended by the church of Christ.

In the fourth place, it is imperative that ethnically identifiable churches learn to live consciously in ecumenical interdependence with churches of other races. For the God and Father of Jesus Christ is not a tribal god, nor a local divinity. His church is the One Holy Catholic Church. It is the avant-garde of the new manhood. In principle and in practice, it must be a microcosm of the peoples of the world. Given her mystery and essence, it has an extraordinary calling in the challenge that race relations present to the world. In practice, local and regional churches tend to deteriorate into bulwarks of tribal pride, into seedbeds of hate toward other groups, into confessionally sealed-in communions. Wherever this is the case, churches have traded the living God for a tribal god, and in doing so have betrayed their own calling as the apostolic and catholic church. But wherever churches have seized hold of their calling—locally, regionally, nationally, universally—they are becoming what they really are, trailblazers of the Kingdom of God, the Kingdom that will come to life whole among all races and all nations.

Chapter Five

The Gospel of Christ
and Racial Ideology in South Africa

A chapter devoted to South Africa is justified by three things. First, nowhere else in the whole world is the challenge presented by race relations so burdensome as there, and nowhere else does the future of a land depend so fully on the question of whether its people are able to work together toward a multiracial society. Secondly, the political leaders of South Africa have consciously rejected the solution of a multiracial society and have opted for both the ideology and practice of apartheid. The political leaders are supported with varying consistency by three of South Africa's major churches, none of them affiliated with the South African Council of Churches. They are the Nederduits Gereformeerde Kerken, the Nederduits Hervormde Kerk of South Africa, and the Gereformeerde Kerk of South Africa (the Dutch Reformed Churches, the Dutch Reformed Church of South Africa, and the Reformed Church of South Africa). In these churches, the ideology of apartheid generally comes garbed in the authority of the divine Word. It is this divine endorsement of apartheid that puts the Christian church in the crucible. And this is the reason why in this book we are compelled to oppose the Gospel to nationalist or racist

ideology, and to join forces with individuals in these and
other churches who have rejected and who carry on a
valiant struggle against apartheid.

The third reason is that, in a book written initially for
Dutch readers, confrontation with the ideas of a people
related to them by both language and blood cannot be
avoided, though it may cost some pain. Those white
Afrikaners who settled and developed South Africa were
some of my early heroes, and I still believe that this
remarkable people can make an invaluable contribution
to the reformation of society in South Africa if they will
only listen to the voices of some of their own sons and
daughters. What I want to do in these pages is to translate
some of these voices, and to lend them some support. I
believe in my heart that what I write here is constrained
by the love of Christ, because I am convinced that the
way the tensions between the Gospel and nationalist
ideology in South Africa are handled in the coming years
is going to have enormous consequences not only for the
people in the southern part of Africa, but for people all
over the world.

THE IDEOLOGICAL BASIS OF APARTHEID

The politics of apartheid is open to inspection from
many vantage points. Dr. Ben Marais and several others
have studied it in its social-psychological dimensions, as
in Marais' book *The Two Faces of Africa*. The United
Nations' Unit on Apartheid has published several pieces
in which the politics of apartheid are judged in terms of
norms set down in the U.N.'s "Declaration on Rights of
Men." The International Labor Organization in Geneva
gives out regular reports on the social-economic aspects
of apartheid. The three Dutch scholars G. A. Kooy, W.
Albeda, and R. C. Kwant have demonstrated, in their
book *Apartheid en Arbeidsbestel in Zuid-Afrika (Apartheid and the Labor System in South Africa)* that apartheid is in fact running flatly counter to the social-

economic realities of South Africa and is on this account alone economically as well as socially impracticable.

But what I am interested in is the theological-ethical dimensions of the race question, and I want therefore to concentrate on the fact that in the background of the politics of apartheid lies an ideology which, though whitewashed with the phrase "Christian-national," is not only in treacherous tension with the Gospel, but contradicts wholesale the message of the Bible on race relations.

Ideologies create blueprints for the future of a society, stamped out by human wisdom or human folly as the case may be; they give birth to vast complexes of long-range programs, directives, laws, and definitions whose purpose is to translate the blueprints into social structures. Ideologies often wear a pseudo-religious garb, especially when the policy-makers identify their blueprints and their own application of them with the will of God.

The National Party of South Africa came to power in 1948 and has controlled the country effectively since then under the successive regimes of Malan, Strijdom, Verwoerd, and Vorster. The 1970 election ended with the following alignment of the parties in parliament:

National Party .... 117 seats
United Party .... 47 seats
Progressive Party .... 1 seat
Restored National Party .... no seats

Nonwhites are kept outside the electorate. Whites have complete control of the power-monopoly, and executive control has for twenty years been in the hands of the party which drew up the blueprints for a society rooted solidly in the ideology of apartheid. The National Party looks back to 1948 as the birthdate of a completely new era in the development of South Africa. The nonwhites, of course, but many whites as well, look back to 1948 as the year that set South Africa on a course that will gradually lead it into enormous difficulties, if not complete disaster.

How can we explain the confidence and conviction
that both political and church leaders appear to have
when they proclaim the promising future of South Africa? They can be explained by the fact that the policy of
apartheid is *driven* by an ideology, an ideology that
increasingly shows signs of being a pseudo-religion, which
in turn is creating its own myths, rituals, ethos, and cult.

Let us see if we can locate some of the foundation
stones of the South African nationalist house.

A. *The Afrikaner Brotherhood*

The Afrikaner Brotherhood, which has from the beginning been a powerful factor in the rise of the National
Party, was organized in Johannesburg after World War I,
in 1918. It is a secret organization and is content to stay
behind the scenes. I am not particularly interested in the
history of its movements, but we must note two basic
motives at work in it, both of them ideological in character. First, there is what the Brotherhood itself speaks of
as the Christian-National motif. For the Brotherhood this
motif implies a "separate African nation" incarnating
the "Western-Christian culture" to which God has given,
by divine commission, a dominating role to play in history. As one looks into the vision that guides the Brotherhood, he is constantly struck by how the ideology and
the nationalism tend always to control its avowedly
Christian dimensions.

In the second place, there is the notion of guardianship
over the nonwhite "categories of the population." Guardianship implies that the whites will foster and guarantee
to the nonwhite groups the right to "indigenous development"—within limits. In actual practice, guardianship involves the creation of a racial caste system that guarantees to the whites a monopoly on all political power and
guarantees to the nonwhites a subordinate and inferior
status in the structure of society. The whole concept of
guardianship rests on white supremacy.

These two basic motifs—Christian Nationalism and

guardianship—help us understand how the National Party, supported by the Afrikaner Brotherhood, manages to continue to attract broad support from the white electorate. On the one hand, it wins the support of that segment of the population which simply and crudely wants to "keep the Bantus in their place." On the other, it wins those who genuinely want to do something for the nonwhite—a great deal, perhaps, or maybe at least a little—but who nonetheless look on the nonwhites as their charges, inferiors whom they could not accept as fellow members within the fabric of their society.

The Afrikaner Brotherhood finds itself just now in a serious crisis, a crisis resulting from the fact that the two minds we just mentioned are at odds with each other within the Brotherhood. In this crisis, the *Restored* National Party is asserting itself. The splenetic efforts of this party, led by Albert Hertzog, son of the famous General Hertzog, won it no seats in the most recent election, but its ultra-reactionary approach has created a serious split in the Afrikaner Brotherhood, leaving the Brotherhood in a state of mutual distrust as the contest for control develops. The younger people have been pretty much alienated; among youth there is now very little interest in this secret organization. One gets the impression that the Brotherhood is preparing for its own funeral. Not only is there a lot of intra-Brotherhood mistrust, but the extremists are arousing skepticism in the minds of some about the Christian-Nationalist ideology that lies at its source. Some South Africans are sensing that Christianity and Western culture cannot be equated, and that maybe the sacralizing of the African nation has introduced false altars into the temple. Yet, while the new skepticism is real, the dreams and hopes born of the pseudo-religious ideology of the Afrikaner Brotherhood still dominate the mind of the South African leadership.

During World War II, white Afrikaners were sharply divided as to whether South Africa should remain neutral or support the Allies. Many whites supported Field Marshal Jan Smuts in the war against Hitler, and distinguished themselves. Others, among whom was Dr. Malan, believed that South Africa's calling was to remain neutral. But there was a third group. It was a semi-military organization called Die Ossewabrandwag. Led by such men as the present prime minister, John Vorster, this group engaged in sabotage against the Smuts troops, which were committed to the struggle against the Nazis. After the war, when more of the grotesque features of National Socialism became undeniable even in South Africa, the activities of the Ossewabrandwag were not a subject South Africans liked to talk about. But it must be recorded that the ideology of the Ossewabrandwag was Nazist, pure and simple.

A sampling of Ossewabrandwag ideology is found in a document dated 1944, written by Dr. J. A. H. van der Walt and published by the Cultural and Information Service of the Ossewabrandwag. The document is described as containing the Basic Principle adopted by the "Great Council of the Ossewabrandwag." Dr. van der Walt called it the "political creed" of the organization and introduced it with a sentence that makes the National Socialist motif explicit. I will let the document speak for itself:

> We recognize that the health of our national political life lies only with a nationalism that is socialistic and with a socialism that is nationalistic. Only thus will right be done, in reference to the past as well as the future, to the generations gone by and to those yet to come.
>
> a. The party structure must give way to an organization that will unite the people in an all-embracing People movement. It must embrace the family, but with it the various labor groups, culture groups, and the entire national order. Thus, we shall gather all the power of the people within one totality for the support and security of the Republic.
>
> b. The present parliamentary, provincial and municipal governments must be replaced by a powerful and qualified

central authority that embraces all sections of the country, an authority that will include true representatives from both the people and from every vocational sphere representing every interest.

c. The various vocations must be set in shape to put their own houses in order and to control their affairs under the coordinated direction of the State and in cooperation with the People movement.

d. Citizenship will be restricted to those who either now belong to the people or are potential members—that is, those whites who prove themselves assimilable. Citizenship will be possible for Europeans as well as for present Afrikaans- and English-speaking citizens. But privilege of citizenship depends on unswerving fidelity to the fatherland. All other white persons will be given only the right of guests and not of citizenship.

e. Non-whites will be restricted to non-white areas, for the advance of racial purity and the racially pure development of all segments of the society, consistent, of course, with proper respect to needs for labor.

f. Afrikaner-hood accepts its responsibility to lead the "Christian-national development" of South Africa in association with those Western Cultural Forces and the related white peoples whose interests are parallel to our own, *particularly in the New Europe*!

g. The Christian-national development of our own people, and of both the colored and naturals [blacks] who live within our borders, shall be secured in full cooperation with recognized Christian churches, by outlawing all provocative propaganda, racial mixing and race hatred, by control of all the propaganda media, and by a thorough reforming of the schools along Christian-national lines, for all segments of the population.

h. Public welfare will be concentrated on sound family life and productive industry. Unemployment will not be tolerated, and employers will be tied into the national life so as to prevent any uncertainties in labor's productivity of the necessities of life.

i. The sources of production will be put under the direction of the government, in the first instance through the private initiative of the citizens, developed wholly in the national interests, and the wealth thus produced will be equitably divided between the various participants in the production process.

j. Capitalism, with its anti-nationalist leadership, particularly in the case of mining, factories, commerce, and finance, will be abolished; prices, profits, and indebtedness will be controlled; speculation in land, building, consumables, and clothing will be prevented. Godless and race-less communism will be supplanted by a biblical and native socialism.

This document hardly needs commentary. It is a typical specimen of National-Socialist ideology. Its influence in South Africa during the war years was greater than will be admitted today. And it is also undeniable that the Ossewabrandwag was the semi-military arm of the Afrikaner Brotherhood.

It would, however, be untrue to say that all members of the Afrikaner Brotherhood and the leadership of the National Party swallowed this ideology whole. Dr. Malan, who led the National Party in those days, kept himself aloof from these ideological excesses, and indeed cautioned against them, as he did against the excesses of the Nazis. But it is a fact of history that the Nazi ideology was accepted, even lauded, by many and that its ferment is still at work in South Africa.

B. The Ideological Ferment Within the National Party

We should add some notes taken from the speeches and papers of the architects of the politics of apartheid. It was Dr. Malan who worked out the politics of forced segregation and published them in a political manifesto. On election evening, April, 1938 (ten years before the National Party gained power), Malan read a party manifesto on apartheid that was eventually to mean a radical change for the "naturals"—the term used at the time for black Africans, since then officially changed to "Bantus." Malan's manifesto follows:

> a. The Party favors the revision of our existing laws respecting the Naturals [Bantus] to the end that the voting rights of the Naturals for the Parliament and the Cape Provincial Council be ended, that migration of Naturals to urban areas be prevented, the entire change to effect the eventual removal of the Naturals from the cities and their segregation in prescribed areas.
>
> b. The Party intends to end the present large-scale purchase of land for Naturals by the State, and to allow the purchase to be made at the private initiative of the Naturals in keeping with their real needs.
>
> c. The Party intends further to pursue the consistent application of the principle of segregation in respect to all non-whites, as being in the best interests of the whites as well as the non-white races, and intends for that purpose to introduce legislation that will provide for:
>
> (1) separate living areas, separate labor organizations, and, as far as is workable, separate places of employment for whites and non-whites;
>
> (2) provision of employment opportunities in certain trades for whites only, and fixed and fair employment quotas for whites and non-whites;
>
> (3) separate representation in our legislative bodies for the coloreds of the Cape area who now have voting rights; and
>
> (4) the expansion of the "immorality act" of 1926 to include *all* non-whites, for the prevention of mixed marriages as well as the prohibition of employment of whites by non-whites.

This is a most revealing manifesto, if only because it brought into the open the union between racist and nationalistic ideology. The National Party's politics are concentrated on the security and power of the "white race"; the reduction of nonwhite rights was obviously directed to that end. The manifesto also makes it clear that the National Party wanted to introduce a racial caste system in which each group would be given a prescribed amount of room to maneuver, but in such a way as to guarantee white monopoly on power and the subordination of all interests to the white population.

It took ten years for the National Party to succeed in translating this manifesto into concrete political action. But the time did come, and the National Party immediately upon gaining power began to apply the manifesto to national life.

One point of the manifesto, the one calling for the purchase of land for the Bantus, was discarded. Aside from this, the ideological game-plan was follow *in toto*— particularly after the Tomlinson Report appeared. This report was the work of the Tomlinson Committee (named after its chairman, the agricultural expert Prof. T. L. Tomlinson), which was appointed by the government in 1950 with the mandate to draw up a blueprint for enforced segregation on the basis of apartheid ideology. The report was laid on the table in 1954 by way of a series of eighteen sections. While not every recommendation was adopted, it was accepted in all of its main provisions.

It was Dr. Hendrik Verwoerd who in the course of his political rise was most prominent in working out the plan for separate development. Some of the important segments of the speeches in which he developed his program appeared in W. A. Landman's book *A Plea for Understanding*. It is clear from these, in the first place, how Verwoerd worked out of a nationalistic interpretation of history:

> For what purpose and reason should whites have been led to the Southern region of Africa 300 years ago? Why has this small group been blessed with such growth as to have spread all over Africa? For what purpose did they endure

> their struggles to survive as a people? I believe that all this
> has a purpose. The purpose is this, that we should form the
> bulwark for Western civilization in Africa.

This shows Verwoerd's sense of historical destiny for the
whites; one finds the same dogma of white supremacy in
all his speeches and the same self-assured faith that the
maintenance of a white monopolistic power structure is a
response to divine calling. Wilson and Thompson, in their
Oxford History of South Africa, Vol. I, have convincingly
shown that this view of historical destiny is full of myths
and is precisely calculated to prevent people of differing
points of view from taking roles in the political life of a
nation.

In the second place, one is impressed how Dr. Verwoerd presents his political program of segregated development with Gospel-like unction. "The purpose," he
proclaims,

> must be set forth with clarity. The politics of separate
> development is the foundation for the happiness, the secu-
> rity and the stability that can be maintained only when each
> group has its own homeland, its own language, and its own
> rule; and it holds for the Bantus as well as for the whites. I
> am for apartheid, not only for whites and blacks, but for
> the colored, for the Indian people, the Chinese, the Malay-
> sians; and I am for advancing apartheid even to the various
> tribes.

Again and again, Verwoerd identifies his ideology of
separate development under white supervision with the
will of God.

C. *The Theological Justification of Apartheid*

Some theologians of the three churches that support
apartheid are distinguished for devoting their talents to
provide apartheid a theological justification. It is sometimes supposed that Afrikaners believe they have been

called to fill the role that Israel played in the Old Testament. But this is wrong. The notion may have been alive
at the time of the Afrikaners' great migration to the
North and even among the founders of the Boer Republic, and it may even be semi-conscious in the popular
self-image, but I know of no theologian who would care
to defend this. Nor does the notion that blacks are the
doomed children of Ham find any defenders in South
African circles. But this does not mean that there is no
theological probing for religious foundations to support
the racial caste system. The ingredients of this religious
foundation come down, I think, to something like this:

(1) Theologians in the Dutch Reformed Church contend that the Bible teaches that the differences between
races are as fundamental as are the unity of humanity,
redemption in Christ, and the restoration of unity in
Him. As we have seen, this is really a pseudo-theology.
The concept of race does not even appear in the Bible in
the sense that we think of races today. Racial and ethnic
differences are not cast by "creation ordinances." Racial
differences are phenomena that arose in the course of
history; they vary, change, shift in ways that do not even
touch the unity of the human race. Anyone starting with
the thesis that the difference between races is "just as
important" as the unity and the restoration of that unity
falls into a racial ideology which can only lead to racist
ethics and a racist credo.

(2) An interpretation of the tower of Babel forms
another ingredient in apartheid ideology. It holds that
this story teaches that God's will is seen in the division of
the people into separated communities. This interpretation, however, simply does not touch down on reality. It
ignores the fact that this story is not the final word
regarding God's intention for men, not by a long shot.
God's real intentions are revealed in the appearance of
the ecumenopolis, the New Jerusalem as envisioned in
Revelation 21. And His intention is clear in the commission to us to follow the lines that point in that direction.

(3) An interpretation of Paul's speech to the Athenians forms another ingredient. It hinges on Paul's statement that God "defined the borders of their habitation" (Acts 17:26). The Areopagus speech, however, is a powerful attack against racial rites, myths, and ethos as fostered among the Greeks. How it is possible to extract from Paul's words any justification for whites to make arbitrary decisions as to where black people may live would be a question too ridiculous to bother with if the real life of so many people were not actually at stake.

Systems like those developed in South Africa, racial caste systems, have not been rare in world history. But it is seldom that such systems have been defended in the name of Christ. It is remarkable that the name of Him who came to break down the walls between races should be used to justify building the walls again. Amazing, that He who came to integrate human beings into one body should be used to form the cornerstone of a totally segregated society. Surely, the name of Jesus Christ is prostituted here.

APARTHEID IN PRACTICE

No one can deny that within the framework of apartheid a good deal of good has been done for the nonwhite groups. The sloppy administration of the Smuts era, when everything was left to run its own course, is done with. Edgar Brookes, a bitter opponent of apartheid, acknowledges in his *Three Letters from Africa* that during the twenty years that Jan Smuts dominated the political scene, the nonwhites were both bullied and ignored by the government and pretty much left to their fate. This is no longer true. They are not bullied and they are not ignored. But they are manipulated. And there is no detergent that can wash away the fact that the entire apartheid policy is rooted in a Herrenvolk ideology that has grown up into a racially defined caste system whose goal is to guarantee white monopoly of the power structure.

Objective information on the laws regulating apartheid and the implementing of the laws is available. Almost everything can be picked up in a brief and terse account found, without commentary, in the little book *Legislation and Race Relations,* put together by Muriel Horrell and published in a revised edition by the Institute for Race Relations in 1966. In what follows, I want to try to expose the inner linkage between the ideology and the practice of apartheid. It is not my intention to report all the details of the laws and their application. Ideology results in action; one first thinks, then speaks, and then acts—at least this is how South African apartheid evolved. One must judge the tree by its fruits. And the fruits of this ideology are sour.

A. *Political Apartheid*

In 1950, the population of South Africa was divided into racial categories by means of an elaborate system of classification (Population Registration Act No. 30). Identification cards were issued to every person to indicate his racial category. In 1959 and in 1962, the classifications were honed down to more precise categories. In the same year, the government issued a law for the "promotion of Bantu self-government." The intent of the law was to make it impossible for the Bantus to participate in the central government. To achieve this, representation from the Bantus, which before that time allowed for the election of four Bantu senators to the parliament, was eliminated. Representation from other nonwhite racial categories was also eliminated. The result was that the central government consisted exclusively of whites. All nonwhite categories were then reduced to very limited representation in *advisory* commissions (separate ones for each category, e.g., the Colored and the Indian, as well as the Bantu).

These regulations meant the elimination of any interracial political organization. The Liberal Party, for example, of which Edgar Brookes and Alan Paton were spokesmen, was effectively eliminated. They also meant the elimination of the larger black political organizations, such as the African National Congress in which Albert Luthuli, Professor Matthews, and later Nelson Mandela and Walter Sisulu worked, and the Pan African Congress, the party of Robert Sobukwe.

The bloodbath of Sharpeville, on March 28, 1960, exposed the scandalous fact that the blacks in the urban centers had no organ through which to express their grievances, let alone fight to overcome them. The government's response to the massacre ignored the causes of the grievances: the government reacted simply by prohibiting the only two political organizations the blacks had. The black Africans henceforth enjoyed political rights exclusively in their prescribed segregated territories. The leaders of the black parties and other organizations were exiled, put in prison, or politically ostracized from the community. The Sabotage Act inflicted the death penalty on all acts of sabotage. The infamous 180-Day Law meant detention without any legal process. And the Anti-Terrorism Act gave the government the power to extend any detention of a person indefinitely. The military and police apparatus for the maintenance of order was expanded broadly. A secret service, swarming with police informers, gained control of civil life.

Edgar Brookes, the well-known historian of law at Rhodes University who represented the Bantus in the Senate for many years, wrote: "We eliminated from any place in the central government all men of dignity and moderation, like the late Luthuli and Matthews; if we continue on this course, we will lose all chance of dealing with reasonable men like these and shall have to deal with demagogues and dictators." He recalled the words of Jesus: "Make friends quickly with your accuser, while you are going with him to court, lest your accuser hand you over to the judge, and the judge to the guard, and you be put in prison" (Matt. 5:25).

The warning is not pious jargon. To withhold political rights from the majority of the populace or to offer them make-believe rights without actual participation in the central government, to imprison the representatives of the majority or to ban and harass them is eventually to commit suicide. Brookes concluded with an impassioned plea for South Africa to awaken from its dreamworld of apartheid and to establish genuine political rights for all the people of the land.

B. Territorial Apartheid

Territorial apartheid has been uppermost in the design of South Africa since the birth of apartheid ideology. Territorial apartheid comes down to this: First, the white group, with its monopoly on power, arbitrarily and unilaterally divides the land, and second, it determines arbitrarily and unilaterally which sections shall be set aside as Bantustans (i.e., homelands, or reservations) for particular ethnic segments of the population.

Some South Africans recall the arrangement that Abram made with Lot in Genesis 13. We read there that the two men, uncle and nephew, agreed *voluntarily* to separate, and that they looked over the land *together*, and that Lot received the best land. But the directors of apartheid never looked out over the land together with the others. They decided by themselves, arbitrarily, that the land should be divided. Then they decided, following the recommendations of the Tomlinson Report, that 13 percent of the land be allotted the Bantus and that 87 percent of the land be given to the whites. The following reservations were to be designated: Transkei (already effected), Ciskei, Zululand, Tswanaland, the Northernmost areas, and Southern Sotho—all to be divided between the eight major groups of Bantus.

Fundamental to this plan are the Bantu Authorities Act of 1951 and the Bantu Self-Government Act of 1959. Transkei is the first designated area in which the plan is being worked out. In 1963 the Transkei area received self-government. The political arrangement allows the traditional tribal heads to have a majority representation, and thereafter the representatives of the various political parties are given minority role. Bantus who count the Transkei their homeland but who are employed outside the Transkei have no political rights in the place where they actually live; their rights are limited to their officially designated homeland, which, however, is not their place of residence. The intention is to get the Bantus all back to their designated reservations, to live and work there.

The purpose of territorial apartheid is clear. This policy means that the great ethnic groups will be eliminated from all participation in the total development of South Africa and that the blacks will be subject to manipulation by the white minority for the sake of white supremacy, white racial purity, and white economic security. But all the while the real purposes are camouflaged with ideological rationalization.

The most consistent attempt to justify territorial apartheid was made by Prof. J. H. Coetzee of the *Word and Deed* group in Potchefstroom. He wrote a paper that he titled "The South African Concept of Homeland in the Context of Separate Development." It was read on March 18, 1970, in Potchefstroom, and it is a typical specimen of many efforts to wrap apartheid in ideological justification. Coetzee uses semantics to locate the origin of the word *gebied* (territory) in the word *gebod* (commandment), and uses this semantic oddity to argue that separate reservations are really a response to a divine command. Along with this, apologists for territorial apartheid, like Coetzee, plead for a more consistent working out of the territorial idea. There is, Coetzee complains, still too much dealing in snippets; other than the Transkei, plans for the several special reservations have not materialized. So, he says: "The black enclaves must be rooted out of white areas," and "black colonies within the cities

that were created by whites must be eliminated." Of
course, the question of whether the "black colonies" will
cooperate with their own removal from the cities is a
matter that gives the ideologists and bureaucrats a "big
headache." But the question of whether their removal
will cause the "black colonies" a "big headache"—personally or socially—appears to be of minor consequence. The
consolidation of the reservations, say the ideologues,
must now be attacked with renewed vigor.

The fact that the large ethnic groups are actually
composites of smaller ethnic groups also creates a problem. But, it is said, the task is to *develop* the inhabitants
of the reservations *into* united people or nations; the
actual ethnic divisions must be ignored so that the process of *forming* a people for each reservation can be
pressed forward. While secularization is in fact leading
toward detribalization, apartheid ideology runs against
this trend as it tries to create tribes and to reshape them
into political unities.

The working out of territorial apartheid does not solve
any of the economic problems, and this is well known to
the apartheid ideologists. But this fact is only accepted as
a challenge. The purpose must be gradually to force all
blacks to their respective reservations. "We should never
expect," says Coetzee, "that people will be loyal to a
land they must leave in order to make a living." Thus, it
is urged, the economic development of the reservations
must be stimulated so that the Bantus will in some
distant future day be able to work and live in their own
places.

The critical question is whether carrying the apartheid
ideology into practice will involve the sacrifice of hun-
dreds of thousands of people to a morally repugnant and
practically impossible ideology. This question is never put
on the agenda, nor is it ever discussed in papers like that
delivered by Coetzee.

I cannot, within the limits of this book, begin to give a
complete account of the harsh realities introduced by

territorial apartheid. But it may be valuable to mention a few invaluable sources of information in which the real and persistent human question is not evaded.

In her book *The African Reserves* (1969) Muriel Horrell gives an objective report on the development of the reservations, and in her annual review of race relations she shows how the territorial plan has developed from year to year. She goes into all facets of life in the reservations and draws some conclusions. For instance, she concludes that the policies stimulate rather than diminish tribal loyalties. It strengthens rather than weakens the role of the autocratic tribal chiefs, and thus holds back any trend toward more democracy within tribes. Territorial apartheid also means that the Bantus living in white-controlled urban areas are existing in a political no-man's land at the same time that their paper rights within their reservations are meaningless to them.

The health situation in the Transkei is deplorable in spite of the good work done by hospitals there, and the reason is that the economy of the reservations is in incredibly bad shape. The government of the Transkei reported in 1969 that harvests there have not improved at all in thirty years. The Xhosa Development Corporation has neither sufficient capital nor know-how to get the economy on its feet. The so-called "border industries" just inside the border of white areas and organized to attract black laborers out of their reservation are no solution at all to the people of the Transkei for the simple reason that they exist 250 miles away from Transkei, and this means that Transkei men who work in them do so as migrant workers. The regulations set out in the legislation of 1968 to encourage Afrikaans or English investors to take some initiative in Transkei have until now been unsuccessful. The general condition in the reservations is grotesquely bad, an inevitable result of the whole system.

Less statistical, but a book made authentic by its eyewitness accounts of the tragic reality, is *The Discarded*

People, written by Cosmas Desmond, O.F.M. Published in 1970 by the Christian Institute in Johannesburg, it provides an account of the relocation of old people and children from the white-dominated areas to the relocation areas designated by the territorial legislation. The ideologues tell us that certain segments of the people *have* to be relocated, for whatever reason. Desmond, who knows these people intimately, many by name, tells us how the relocation is actually done and how the people suffer through it. The question is, Why must people live so miserably in a land so fabulously rich? Things that happened all over the world in the 19th century, but that are simply unthinkable in the seventh decade of the 20th century are actually happening now in the richest country of Africa. The apologia for apartheid, says Desmond, is blasphemy. Can it really be *God's* will that whites should buy their security with what is happening in the Transkei, in Morsgat, in Weenan, and in Morzeshas? "When homeland freedom is promised to the nonwhites, it smells of fraud; when we are asked to believe that the present situation in South Africa makes freedom there possible, it smells of fantasy." Let's be frank: even the creators of this political scheme know it is fantasy.

Understandably, resistance to being shut up in a reservation (euphemistically called their "homeland") is growing among the Bantus. There is also growing resistance to being shut off from all real participation in the total development of the South African republic. Resistance is strongest among the thousands of Bantus who exist at present in the social-political no-man's land within the "townships" set inside the urban areas; these people know better than most how impossible the notion of a "homeland" or reservation is.

C. The Colored People in the Cape Province and the Indians in Durban

Territorial apartheid assumes that it is possible to mark off distinct territories as the original homelands of specific peoples, quite apart from whether the people are in fact really matched with their real homelands. But there are groups within South Africa for whom it is clearly impossible to locate this sort of a separate "homeland." These are the "Coloreds" from Cape Province and the Indians in Durban and Pietermaritzburg.

The strange name "Colored" refers to the large group of people, living mostly in West and East Cape Province, who stem from a mixture of the whites with the original inhabitants of South Africa. These are the people sometimes called Hottentots and Bush People (who speak Khoikoi or San), whom Van Riebeeck met in the Cape. Along with these (whites and original dwellers) came slaves imported from Malaysia and the Indian Archippoles. The "Colored," then, stem from *original* South Africans, as they were mixed with whites and a small minority of others. They have the same homeland as do the whites. They are people who helped create the beautiful language called Afrikaans; they now speak either Afrikaans or English, share the same religion as do the majority of whites, namely Calvinism (though there are a small minority of Moslems), and share the same Afrikaner culture. What, then, of the "Coloreds"?

D. P. Botha, in his impressive book on the Colored people of the Cape, *The Rise of a Third Class*, defends the thesis that the Colored have from the very beginning been an integral part of the same new society established by Van Riebeeck. "Whenever we all needed them, they were one with us, even to the death." This was true in the Boer War and in the war with the Zulus during Piet Retief's great trek northward.

In 1960, 370,000 Coloreds were found alongside 300,000 whites. This group, which since the coming of Dutchmen, English, Huguenots, and other Westerners has formed an identifiable community, is now beginning to feel the whole brunt of apartheid. Dr. Malan was at first for integrating this community within the Republic. But after 1938 he was of another mind. Once the National

Party gained power, forced segregation was applied to the
Coloreds as to the Bantus.

Social segregation for the Colored began in 1948. The
freedom of movement taken for granted by them since
the initial settlement is now denied. They may no longer
share the same compartment with whites on South African trains. The famous Immorality Act controls all their
sexual relations. Housing laws specify where they may
live. Educational facilities are separate and discriminatory
against them. The "laws of segregation have meant for
this group a massive and painful dislocation," says Botha.

The policies of apartheid do concede certain political
rights to the Coloreds; they can take part in what is called
the "Colored Council." But they are denied a share in the
Central government, though the first elections for the
Colored Council in 1950, and again in 1969, have made it
perfectly clear that the mass of Coloreds oppose apartheid.

The separation is visible in the churches too. The
Dutch Reformed Church and the Dutch Reformed Colored Church are known, maternalistically, as the Mother
and Daughter churches.

Botha makes a passionate plea for integration between
whites and Colored communities. He describes the Colored as the "natural partner and potential friend of
whites." And he warns that if the government does not at
once make a complete and radical turnabout in its segregation policy toward the Colored, all we can expect is the
shedding of blood, "an event that will break our heart."

I mention Botha's book because, of all who have
written on the Colored question, he has lived with and
known the Colored community since childhood and has
given his life and work to it in a most inspiring way. What
I cannot comprehend about Botha's position is that while
he pleads for integration between Colored and white, he
is on the side of apartheid for the Bantus. Had he grown
up among the Bantus instead of among the Coloreds,
would he not have discovered among them the same

desire for justice, the same hope for participation and integration within the Republic? If Botha's position were accepted, would it not lead to a situation in which the whites try to embrace the Coloreds on their side in the conflict of interests over against the Bantus, and would not the Coloreds then become a football kicked around between whites and blacks? In short, ought not men like Botha fight for integration and participation for *all* the groups of South Africa?

What applies to the Coloreds applies as well to the Indians in Durban and Pietermaritzburg, a people totalling around 600,000. They have no distinct homeland anyone . could point to. Before apartheid, this community had advanced itself on all fronts, economic, social, and cultural, and it is quite self-conscious of its identity and its accomplishments. This is as true of the Hindus and Moslems as it is of the Christians among them. But now their life as a people, too, is restricted narrowly within the framework of apartheid, and they must play their role as second- or third-class citizens. I can well understand a remark a certain Moslem leader made to me: "In our 'homeland,' India, the caste system was officially eliminated; here in South Africa we have a racial caste system established in the name of the same Christianity that dug the grave of the caste system in India. Must we not conclude that defense of the South African system has got to be essentially quite anti-Christian?"

D. Apartheid and Labor Relations

Information about the effects of apartheid on labor relations is not hard to come by. Let me mention just a few sources. J. A. Grobbelaar, who is general secretary of TUCSA (the Trade Union Council of South Africa), gave a speech in 1968 about the labor movement and the economic future of South Africa that is a treasure of information, some of which has been published by the Institute for Race Relations. In 1964, the ILO (International Labor Organization) instructed its director to publish yearly reports on labor relations in South Africa, and these reports have appeared annually since then, giving a thorough account of events. Professors Kooy, Albeda, and Kwant have put together a book with the title, *Apartheid en Arbeidsbestel in Zuid-Afrika (Apartheid and the Labor System in South Africa)*. The monthly magazine *Outlook* carries regular pieces by Francis Wilson on the subject.

Let me make a few summary remarks, some gathered from such sources as I have mentioned, some from conversations and firsthand observation.

(1) The Bantus are permitted to organize unions, but their unions may not be registered in white territories and have absolutely no right to engage in collective bargaining or to call strikes. Strikes are absolutely forbidden all nonwhite workers.

(2) Equality of opportunity in work is nonexistent. The labor-reserve laws protect the white worker against competition from the black, and exclude blacks from specific forms of employment. This system of labor-reserve was introduced in 1956 along with the Law for Industrial Conciliation. This is a law that gives the Minister of Labor the authority to prevent certain types of industry within certain areas. In 1969 the Bantu Laws Amendment Bill was added, giving the Minister of Labor even more authority. In 1970 one of the ministers proposed that all Bantus living in cities be excluded from all "middle-class functions"; this would prevent any Bantu from working as a store clerk, telephonist, typist, and the like. The bill is before parliament as this is written.

(3) There is an appaling inequity in wages. Wherever economics compels whites to employ Bantus in the same kind of work as whites do, there is not even a gesture of equality in payment. Bantu wages are often one-sixth or one-seventh of white wages in the same job. But in the sections where only blacks are employed, the discrepancy is far worse. The number of black workers is, of course, far larger than the number of whites—four times more

blacks than whites belong to the labor force. And so the blacks are open to exploitation; cheap black labor in South Africa reminds one of the situation in Europe before the rise of labor unions. In fact, South Africa scorns all the norms of organized labor.

(4) In the so-called "border industries," labor organizations are not permitted at all. Here the field for exploitation of blacks is unlimited.

(5) That apartheid, in ideology and in practice, creates a racial caste system is demonstrated in labor relations more clearly than anywhere else.

(6) The only solution to the caste system is the elimination of apartheid and a move toward integration, socially and economically. Justice for the black workers of South Africa will have to mean at least these things: the acceptance of black workers as equal partners in the determination of labor relations; the acceptance of blacks in management as well as in labor; freedom of vocational choice and the admission of blacks into all trades and professions; black admission into all training programs; the right to organize and to engage in collective bargaining; equal pay for equal work; decent working and living conditions for blacks.

The secretary of TUCSA wrote, back in 1968: "We must accept the fact that black Africans now form the largest and most important segment of our labor force, that they will be the most important and most decisive factor in our economic development in the coming years." A dictatorship of capitalists and managers still prevails in many respects, and apartheid perpetuates this dictatorship. Anyone striving for justice in labor relations in South Africa today will have to fight against this economic dictatorship and strive for a new order in which capital investors, management, and labor are restructured in a new order of justice for labor.

E. Migratory Labor

One of the most inhuman practices of apartheid in South Africa is the system of migratory labor. Thousands

of Bantus are provided work-permits for jobs in cities and
are then forced to live and work there alone, without
their families. They are permitted to visit their families
back in the reservation only a few days each month. The
length of the family reunion is closely regulated, and if a
worker overruns his visit only briefly, his work-permit
can be withdrawn, and with it his last chance to support
his family. This migratory labor system condemns hun-
dreds of thousands of black Africans to exile from their
wives and children, and creates horrible moral and social
problems in its wake.

The Synod of the Dutch Reformed Church published a
report on migratory labor in 1965. The Anglican
Church's Committee on Social Responsibility issued a
statement in 1966. Both reports present a stark picture.
Children and elderly people are plucked out of the city
like deadwood and shipped to their reservation, where
both the young and the very old live without decent and
responsible care. In the cities, where working men live
apart from their families, loneliness leads to prostitution
and to countless illegitimate and unwanted children, and
the anxieties and tensions experienced under the pressure
of these illegal relationships result in widespread violence
among the blacks. And where wives do secretly live with
their husbands, children grow up in an atmosphere of
dread and insecurity; night and day these clandestine
families live in fear of being caught in the act of living as
a family.

Each year Family Day is celebrated as a national holi-
day. On that day, the sacredness and high calling of
family life are touted everywhere as "the foundation for
a stable society." Meanwhile, the official system of migratory labor is destroying the family life of thousands of
people; its very structure tears families apart and forces
their members to pay a horrible price of pain and insecurity to keep white supremacy afloat.

The only answer the authorities have offered to these
conditions, as of now, is to clear the cities of black
people after ten o'clock in the evening. This is the rule,

for instance, in Johannesburg. If a man and his wife both have work-permits in Johannesburg, and arrange secretly to spend a night together in a rented room, they may be broken into by police with orders to separate them forcibly and throw one of the parties into jail. If a man wants that badly to be with members of his family, his only way is to be sent back to the reservation to join the unemployed there.

The Dutch Reformed protest against the *blatant* horrors of migratory labor is commendable. But it makes real sense only if it is joined by protests against the entire system. The authorities could meet the demands of the Dutch Reformed merely by clearing the cities of all blacks, which would only compound the injustice. Protests against the inevitable evil *effects* of the system are futile unless they are part of a protest against the entire apartheid system, of which migratory labor is only one of the most scandalous and tragic symptoms.

The wretched migratory labor system is beginning to be felt in white farming areas also. Traditionally one might find several Bantu families on a white farm; the black father could keep a piece of land in exchange for his labor. This was the so-called "labor-tenant" system. Bantu families in this situation at least lived together as families, and always enjoyed a measure of security within the system. But apartheid legislation has in principle brought this tradition to an end. Bantu men may now work on white farms only on contract. And the other members of the Bantu families are relocated to other areas. And so the destruction of family life continues, leading to the same rotten consequences in the rural areas as in the urban. The same thing is happening among the so-called "squatters"; these are blacks who rent small sections of land from white farmers. These people too are gradually being removed from their farms and forced to relocate in the reservations, from which the men, if they are lucky, begin a new and wretched existence as migratory laborers apart from their families.

Migratory labor means, in effect, that blacks are

robbed of their rights to a normal and healthy family life for one reason—to serve the comforts of whites in their areas. Forty percent of the Bantu men work under these conditions outside of their homeland. The entire system is an anachronism that contradicts every dimension of a responsible social and economic structure. Need we even mention its immorality?

F. Apartheid and Education

Premier Verwoerd and M. C. de Wet Nel, his Minister of Education, laid the groundwork for a system of education that provides for the separate instruction of the different racial categories. The National Party considers its segregated educational system as one of the outstanding achievements of the entire apartheid program. If one counts up the number of schools that have been built within the framework of the system, he has to admit there is reason for pride. But if he goes on to investigate the intentions and motives behind these segregated schools, and if he probes into what actually happens inside them, he has to conclude that the whole system, both in principle and in practice, is shaped and directed by the same objectionable goals that infect every part of the apartheid ideology. Let me enumerate some facets of the system.

(1) Compulsory education does not apply to children of black Africans, although the right to an education is a fundamental human right and although South Africa is economically capable of providing it.

(2) Education is provided free for white children, paid from public funds. Education for Bantu children (in the cities) is paid for largely by the blacks themselves, since public funds made available to them comprise only one-tenth of what is given to white children. Buildings, books, fees for examinations, and the like must be paid for by the parents. Any auxiliary services beyond regular class-room exercises, which the state provides free for whites,

must be paid for privately by black parents. All this means that the lowest rung of the economic ladder bears the heaviest burden if black children are to be educated. In practice it also means that only a small minority of black African children attend school for any appreciable period of their lives.

(3) Entrance into a South African University is extremely difficult for any gifted Bantu. Attendance at a foreign university is not permitted unless the candidate can pass specially designed additional examinations at home. There exists an Association for the Educational and Cultural Advancement of the African People in South Africa whose purpose is to provide special assistance to black Africans who do strive to overcome the entrance hurdles. But the very necessity of this organization serves to underscore the enormous problems that the more gifted blacks must cope with.

(4) The number of black Africans who reach the university level is disproportionate to the black population in South Africa. In 1967, 60,747 white students were enrolled in the universities of South Africa. At the same time, there were 3,320 blacks, 3,191 Indians, and 1,438 Colored.

(5) The education of the Bantus is directed toward retribalization and shuts the minds of black children off from an awareness of the world. The Bantu children are educated to think of themselves and their world only in terms of their own tribes at a time when broad vistas of information are required for young people to learn to live in the modern world, a world that is becoming *one* world.

(6) The whole design of segregated information aims at closing the door for Bantu children to South African and world citizenship. This design is consistent with the constitutional declaration of the first Boer republic (The Orange Free State) of the 19th century: "There shall be no equality between white and black, neither in church nor in society." But the design flagrantly contradicts the Christian vision of the equal worth of all men and the

children of men. The Bantu education laws are lauded in South Africa as a panacea for the racial problem; in fact, they could not be better designed to provoke eventual racial conflict.

G. Social Apartheid

Apartheid is applied not only to the larger areas of life (major apartheid), involving the reservation policy, the housing laws, and the like, but extends into the minutest details of social relationships (minor apartheid). Segregated entrances and exits, separate train cars, and separate taxis, busses, toilets, elevators, and the like, abound. In 1965, the following rules were published in Public Accommodation Law No. 26:

> (1) Attendance at theatres set aside for one race is forbidden for any other race.
> (2) Presence in public buildings and playing fields set aside for one racial group is prohibited for others. Presence of mixed racial gatherings in restaurants or tearooms is prohibited.
> (3) Presence as a guest at a private club intended for other than one's race is prohibited.

It is not against the law for a white family to invite black people into their homes. But no black is permitted to stay overnight in the home of a white family unless he is registered as a domestic employee of that family.

All these minor aspects of apartheid are regulated systematically, just as is major apartheid. Major and minor apartheid are tissues of one flesh. It is an illusion to suppose that minor apartheid will gradually disappear on its own, while major apartheid survives. Major and minor apartheid are Siamese twins of the entire system.

I had the privilege of meeting retired Prof. B. B. Keet on the campus of the University of Stellenbosch in 1970. Dr. Keet has fought the forces of apartheid ideology from their very inception. He said to me then, "You will hear people here talking about major and minor apartheid. But I know of only one kind of apartheid, and that is *ugly* apartheid." Minor apartheid is not only ugly, but anti-Christian. The forced isolation between white and black in South Africa is carried on in the name of a Christianity whose essence is precisely the contrary—not isolation but community, not separation but personal communion.

I have been trying to show the relationship between the ideology and the practice of apartheid. The upshot is that the policy of apartheid is fostered by a nationalist ideology that has no other design than white supremacy, the supremacy of the white Afrikaners in South Africa. Its design is to perpetuate that supremacy forever by tying the nonwhite into a program of development that will be guided, controlled, and protected by the white oligarchy.

How long do South Africans believe they can maintain their Herrentum? How long will it take before they see that their ideology is practically self-defeating and morally indefensible?

The ideology cannot be implemented for long. One look at the relative growth of the population is enough to demonstrate how unworkable the policy is. The census of 1969 gives us these figures:

Black Africans	13,300,000
Whites	3,700,000
Colored	1,900,000
Asians	500,000

At this rate, the proportion in the year 2,000 will be 30 million Bantus versus 5 million whites. How can anyone dream of a successful white-controlled apartheid in the face of these figures.

Other factors will contribute to the death of apartheid. Growing economic integration will spill over the boundaries. Technological development, too, in which South Africa is much involved, will demand more and not fewer interrelationships, more integration and less segregation. Apartheid is going to run amuck against economic and technological realities.

But the system is as morally indefensible as it is practically unworkable. The time is now for all Christians to brand the ideology of apartheid as a pseudo-religious bulwark for a system in whose name the God who is no respecter of persons is brought in to sanctify white supremacy over millions of persons. This brings us to the question of how the churches have stood over against both the ideology and the practice of apartheid.

THE CHURCHES AND APARTHEID

Some of the churches have (with some criticism) supported the apartheid policy from the beginning, notably the Dutch Reformed Church of South Africa, the Dutch Reformed Church, and the Reformed Church of South Africa. On the other hand, most of the member churches of the Council of Churches in Africa, the Roman Catholic Church, and other independent churches, after having first hesitated, have with increasing clarity and tempo resisted apartheid both in its ideology and its practice.

A. Critical Support

The Reformed churches have supported and encouraged apartheid by means of all sorts of declarations. In 1950, two years after the National Party took control, a consultation was called in Bloemfontein to provide the ideology of apartheid with a theological buttress. The key sentence of the declaration issued by the conference is this one:

> God has willed races and nations to live separate from one another, each with its own language, with its own culture, etc., and for this reason the segregation of races within the life of the Christian Church as well as public life which leaves the races intact is not only permissible, but is a Christian duty.

This theme is worked out in many variations in countless declarations and publications.

It would be misleading to suppose that these churches see their role as simply one of providing theological propaganda for apartheid. They have been critical partners of the system. The trouble is that any criticism offered is given in the context of a complete and fundamental acceptance of the direction and structure of the apartheid policy. Criticism is sometimes made of the methods by which apartheid is executed. For instance, the brutal way in which the laws respecting segregated living areas are carried out in certain extreme cases has aroused some protest from these churches. The Dutch Reformed Church has repeatedly pointed out the immoral consequences of migrant labor laws. But the protests have not hindered the government from rigidly pursuing both segregated living and the migrant labor system.

Another criticism the churches have made is that the policy of separate development is not being effected consistently enough and that its practical implications are not being accepted. Dr. Hugo du Plessis has frequently pressed this point in his articles in the journal *Word and Deed*. This group feels that the National Party is too opportunistic. It presses for a *rigorous* separation of the races in order to establish several independent states and to create completely separate economies. And, du Plessis argues, if apartheid is not going to be accepted totally, and brought about in spite of the sacrifices it will demand of the whites, then the entire apartheid policy should be scrapped.

It is not possible here to relate all details. Let us just conclude that the official declarations of the Reformed churches support apartheid, but that there is criticism of the method of application in specific instances on the one hand, and that apartheid is not pursued consistently enough on the other. (The latter criticism comes from the *Word and Deed* group in Potchefstroom.)

Within and outside of these churches, however, a very different trend is making itself felt, a trend toward the rejection of the entire ideology of apartheid and a growing call for a multiracial society.

B. *Rising Resistance to Apartheid*

1. THE PASTORAL LETTER OF THE ROMAN CATHOLIC BISHOPS OF 1952

In his forthright book *The Catholic Church and the Race Question*, Yves Congar has shown how in its history the Catholic Church has leaned in principle toward the theory of superior races, and has been hesitant and often temporizing in its practice. South Africa offers evidence to support this historical thesis. But what is important here is that there is also genuine evidence of change. Back in 1952, the archbishops and bishops of South Africa published a pastoral letter in *The Natal* that takes a strong and unequivocal stand against both the idea and the practice of apartheid. A few key statements from this remarkable pastoral letter, given out at the very beginning of the apartheid era, follow:

> (1) Discrimination based on racial differences is an attack on the rights to human dignity that non-whites have equally with whites.
> (2) Discriminatory laws prevent the exercise of fundamental rights. We call special attention to the disruption of family life.
> (3) Justice demands that non-whites be accorded the opportunity to participate increasingly in the political, economic, and cultural life of our country.

2. THE COTTESLOE CONSULTATION OF DECEMBER, 1960

After black resistance to certain aspects of apartheid was put down in a bloody showdown at Sharpeville and all political activity among the Bantus was revoked, the

World Council of Churches sent Dr. R. Billheimer to South Africa for a series of talks. Earlier, Visser 't Hooft had gone, and later he wrote one of the most profound documents ever published on South Africa. With this background and after much careful groundwork, the consultation at Cottesloe was held, bringing together representatives of the WCC with leaders of the following churches: The Bantu Presbyterian Church of South Africa, the Anglican Church of the Province of South Africa, the United Congregational Church, the Methodist Church, the Dutch Reformed Church of Cape Province, the Dutch Reformed Church of the Transvaal, and the Presbyterian Church. Most of the church delegations were multiracial. Eighty percent of the delegates approved of every section of the declaration; this included delegates from the Dutch Reformed Church. One delegate from the Reformed Church of South Africa informed the consultation that he rejected the declaration as a whole. We will now quote the most crucial portion of the declaration:

> We recognize that all racial groups who permanently inhabit our country are a part of our total population and we regard them as indigenous. Members of all these groups have an equal right to make their contribution towards the enrichment of the life of their country and to share in the ensuing responsibilities, rewards and privileges.
>
> The present tension in South Africa is the result of a long historical development and all groups bear responsibility for it. . . . The South African scene is radically affected by the decline of the power of the West and by the desire for self-determination among the peoples of the African continent.
>
> No one who believes in Jesus Christ may be excluded from any church on the grounds of his colour or race.
>
> There are no scriptural grounds for the prohibition of mixed marriages . . . however . . . due consideration should be given to certain factors that may make such marriages inadvisable.

We call attention once again to the disintegrating effects of migrant labour on African life. No stable society is possible unless the cardinal importance of family life is recognized and, from the Christian standpoint, it is imperative that the integrity of the family be safeguarded.

It is now widely recognized that the wages received by the vast majority of the non-white people oblige them to exist well below the generally accepted minimum standard for healthy living. Concerted action is required to remedy this grave situation.

The present system of job reservation must give way to a more equitable system of labour which safeguards the interest of all concerned.

It is our conviction that the right to own land wherever his is domiciled, and to participate in the government of his country, is part of the dignity of the adult man, and for this reason a policy which permanently denies to non-white people the right of collaboration in the government of the country of which they are citizens cannot be justified.

It is our conviction that there can be no objection in principle to the direct representation of Coloured people in Parliament. We express the hope that consideration will be given to the application of this principle in the foreseeable future.

Reading the declaration of Cottesloe now, a decade later, one is impressed with its overly moderate tone, and, at least in regard to the matter of interracial marriage, its tendency to concede too much. Still, there was a real effort to find one another at Cottesloe, a genuine attempt to demand the minimum that moral principle demanded.

Tragically, this moderate statement was rejected by the synods of the three Reformed churches, which have always supported apartheid. The Dutch Reformed Church and the Reformed Church resigned their memberships in the World Council, an event occasioned in part by the Cottesloe resolutions. It has been argued that these churches left the WCC because of constitutional objections relating to the allegation that the synods of the Cape Province and South Transvaal were technically in error when they joined the WCC without consulting other synods beforehand. It has also been said, however, that *at that time* church law left the synods independent of one another in such matters. I was told by Prof. Keet of Stellenbosch that Verwoerd himself brought pressure on the church leadership after Cottesloe, and that in fact it was Cottesloe that lay at the bottom of the regrettable decision to pull out of the World Council.

One of the delegates of the Dutch Reformed Church at Cottesloe was C. F. Beyers Naudé, at that time the moderator of the synod of Transvaal. Naudé has kept faith with his affirmation at Cottesloe, and to translate his conviction into action joined in the organization of the Christian Institute. The Institute's avowed purpose is to struggle for racial justice in the light of the Gospel and Law of God. On being named the director of the Institute, Naudé appealed to the synod of the Transvaal for continuation of his ministerial status. He was turned down. The reasons the synod gave were: (1) The activities of the Christian Institute would likely lead to conflict with the position of the Dutch Reformed Church on the race question; (2) the Institute was assuming functions that were the exclusive responsibilities of the church.

Obviously, the Institute intended, once the churches had turned their backs on Cottesloe, to take stands that it believed the church should be taking, and to fill a role that in the judgment of this courageous group the church should have been playing. It has been doing this since 1963. One of the many jobs the Institute is doing is in response to a request made by the Association of Independent Churches for help in such areas as theological education, literature, and organization. The independent churches arose at the turn of the century and have grown rapidly. No doubt one of the several motives that led to the formation and growth of these churches was a deep desire for self-expression and escape from domination of any sort. The Rev. Keming, secretary of the association, said to me at Uppsala, "The deepest motive behind all these churches is the longing to be recognized as equal human beings. We have asked help from the Christian Institute because we felt that *these* men and women had learned what the Gospel means by human dignity." It may well be that the work of the Christian Institute, aiming at building a multiracial society in the spirit of the Gospel, will be of greater import for the total future of South Africa than those who ridicule it and try to frustrate its work could possibly imagine.

In May of 1962 *Pro Veritate* was begun, a journal edited initially by B. Engelbrecht and now by W. B. de Villiers in which theologians of all the churches are trying to bring the Gospel to bear on the problems of the church and society in South Africa. The journal is marked by openness and courage plus a readiness to face the problems ecumenically. I cannot help thinking of Bonhoeffer and the Bonhoeffer cult. What some worshippers at the Bonhoeffer shrine do not see is that there are still people, here and now, saying what has to be said and doing what has to be done in hard and dangerous situations. There are people in South Africa, among them the *Pro Veritate* circle, working in the spirit and style of Bonhoeffer. The rest of us must listen to them *now* before their voices too are silenced.

C. The Reformed Ecumenical Synod, Lunteren, 1968

Of the three major Reformed churches, two had been members of the World Council. These two, the Dutch Reformed Church (Nederduits Gereformeerde Kerk) and the Reformed Church (Hervormde Kerk), withdrew after the Cottesloe Consultation. One of these, the Dutch Reformed Church, has been and still is a member of the Reformed Ecumenical Synod. So is the third Reformed church, the Reformed Church of South Africa (which never belonged to the World Council). This left the Reformed Ecumenical Synod the one point of contact between churches outside and major Reformed churches within South Africa. In this situation, the 1968 assembly of the Reformed Ecumenical Synod at Lunteren, the Netherlands, took on special importance.

In view of the fact that the present writer helped write one of the two reports on the South African race situation submitted to this synod, and since what happened there was intensely followed within South Africa, it may serve to clarify what happened at Lunteren if I give an account of it as I saw it. The synod was presented with a majority and a minority report. The minority report was defeated by a vote of thirty to sixteen. After its defeat, a committee was appointed to incorporate segments of the minority within the majority report. This having been done, the majority report was accepted.

The South African press covered the synod widely, and some of them noted, rightly, that both majority and minority reports agreed on one thing, that white supremacy, including the principles underlying apartheid, was rejected. The difference between the reports lay in the measure of concreteness: the minority report condemned apartheid explicitly and the majority report kept its criticism implicit. I have read some South African papers which heralded the acceptance of the majority report as a victory for the principles and practices of apartheid. The clearest example of this is found in the church paper *Die Kerkbode* of October 16, 1968, which ran an article by Dr. J. D. Vorster (brother of the Premier) entitled: "The Dutch Reformed Church Does Not Stand Alone." In view of this distortion, we must examine both reports.

1. THE MINORITY REPORT

The writers of the minority report worked in the conviction that the church has to proclaim the Word of God *concretely* in real situations. The Word has two components: Gospel and Law, the promises and the de-

mands of God. To proclaim the Law, the church must
speak anew in every generation to concrete situations in
concrete words. We felt deeply that the church of our
time could not rest with the repetition of former statements, but was called to draw new biblical guidelines for
the realities of our social, economic, and political situation. We felt that the time had come for the church to
measure the practices, the institutions, and the structures
of our societies with the plumbline of the Law. The issue
of race relations could be no exception, especially now
that it had been thrust into and given high priority on
God's agenda by events in history.

The minority report sketched out, briefly, the frighten-
ing situation and the increasing tensions between the
races in the countries within which member churches
were called to live and work: the United States, Nigeria,
Indonesia, Ceylon, the United Kingdom, the Netherlands,
and South Africa. Today's situation, in these places, in
our time, summoned us, we felt, to speak concretely.

It should be noted that the RES had been preoccupied
with this question for *fifteen years*. Now, after fifteen
years of discussion, the reports of the study committees
were on the agenda for decision. The writers of the
minority report were convinced that if, after all these
years, we did not seize the opportunity to say what had
to be said, we would squander the chance that God had
given us and perhaps would not give us again.

I want to add a few remarks on the content of the
minority report. I will limit myself to those sections that
were most criticized by the South African press.

a. *The biblical basis.* We stressed the unity and
solidarity of the human race, and we tried to show how
this excluded the notion that racial differences were
established by a divine creation ordinance. We contended
that to root racial differences in divine ordination was to
erect a pseudo-biblical fortress for segregation, and
should be exposed by the light of the Law and the
prophets as a false ideology. Along with this, we main-

tained that the examples of the prophets compelled us to speak concretely about today's sins of racial injustice, and that the light of the Word should fall on the institutional and structural supports given to racial sins. We concluded with a discussion of the implications of the Gospel of reconciliation for race relations.

b. *The issue of concreteness.* Several committee members were persuaded that we should let the matter rest with general principles; but others of us, a minority, were convinced that our biblical principles should be followed up with concrete applications to specific sins in race relations, sins that summoned us all concretely to repentance, both individually and structurally. This was the breaking point in the committee's discussions, and required the issuing of two reports.

c. *Dr. Gericke and the World Court.* One of the concrete items in the minority report addressed itself to testimony given before the World Court in the Hague by Dr. J. S. Gericke. Gericke appeared before a public session of the World Court on September 20 and 21, 1963, to testify as an expert on the case of South-West Africa. Dr. Gericke defended all of South Africa's policies in respect to South-West Africa, but in particular defended South Africa's efforts to push its apartheid policy there. The World Court jurists took the occasion to remind Dr. Gericke that apartheid had been condemned by several ecumenical church bodies throughout the world. Dr. Gericke countered this statement by an appeal to the Reformed Ecumenical Synod.

First, he insisted that the entire Dutch Reformed Church has consistently supported the apartheid laws and their implementation by the government. He then went on to suggest that the Dutch Reformed Church was itself supported by the Reformed Ecumenical Synod. It is clear that Dr. Gericke was using the RES to defend his government's apartheid policy before the World Court. At any rate, the Court thought so. The presiding jurist disputed Dr. Gericke's right to use the worldwide Reformed fellowship, and cited a statement by Dr. Keet, a South African whose credentials among the Reformed churches are unquestionable: "It is not only with liberal or communist opinion that we are in conflict, but with all Christian trends that approach the question of race relations from a biblical standpoint. *We are out of step with the universal Christian church.*"

Criticism has been leveled against some of us for bringing the Gericke affair into the report. But his appearance before the Court was a public affair, and it had to be dealt with publicly at the synod whose authority was misrepresented to defend views and practices for which the synod had no intention whatsoever of accepting responsibility.

d. *The Toivo question.* As spokesman for the minority report, I quoted from a speech given by Toivo Herman Ja Toivo, the leader of the independence movement in South-West Africa—the SWAPO. It was from a speech Toivo delivered before the supreme tribunal of Pretoria. The quotation reads as follows:

> Your Honor. We find ourselves here in strange land, subjected to laws made by a people we in South-West Africa consider foreigners. We appear before a judge who is not of our people and who does not know our history. We are overwhelmed with this sense of strangeness as we appear before you here in Pretoria. You have no right to rule over us, you have no right to make laws for us in which we have had not a single word to say. You have no right to treat our land as if it belonged to you nor to treat us as if you were our master. We have always considered South Africa an invader of our land. Now the government of South Africa has again asserted its power by passing a law specially directed toward us, and has even declared the law to be retroactive. The government of South Africa has claimed that it rules over South-West Africa with consent of the people. This is untrue. Our organization is the largest political organization in South-West Africa. We view ourselves as a political party.

Toivo then went on to say that he is opposed to violence, but added: "We find ourselves without a vote in our own land, stripped of the right to express our political convictions." I am not interested now in making a judgment on the decision of SWAPO to take the route of violent resistance. The question of South-West African resistance was not the question we faced at the RES assembly. What I wanted to point out was that Dr. Gericke had used his testimony at the World Court to support a policy of forcing apartheid on South-West Africa, and that this justified Toivo's complaint that he and his fellow South-West Africans were deprived of political voice, subjected to laws passed and enforced by South Africa without consultation of the people of South-West Africa.

One response to the Toivo quotation was that we had given a platform to a "terrorist and a Communist." But Toivo, as I then pointed out, is a Lutheran Christian. And, I added, what we must ask ourselves is why it is that some Christians are driven by despair into terrorism and Communism. Could it be that some Christians in our world are in fact leading others, men like Toivo, into temptation?

e. *The propriety of naming churches.* The minority report proposed that concrete matters be brought to the attention of member churches. Reference was made to the racial components of the relationships between rich and poor nations and to the issue of justice within these relationships. The Church of England's attention was brought to symptoms of racism in England. The Netherlands was addressed with reference to the loveless treatment of migrant workers and relations with people from Suriname and the Antilles. The United States was called to recognize the economic imperialism that lies at the root of much of its race problem. Ceylon, Nigeria, and Indonesia were called to readdress themselves to the repeated eruptions of violence between the ethnic minority and majority in their lands. It has been suggested that the report mentioned these countries only to gain a springboard for an attack on South Africa. The fact is that almost every delegate raised objections to specific references to *his* country; none of them thought we were merely trying to indict South Africa.

Anyway, the report did specify South Africa too; its ideology and its practice of apartheid came in for criticism, along with the numerous specific laws that have institutionalized racism in that land. The laws were well known to anyone abreast of recent history there: the housing laws, the Bantu-Authorities Act, the job reservation laws, the 180-Day Law, the law prohibiting interracial marriage, the laws depriving Bantus of participation in political decision-making, and so on.

The Indonesian delegation suggested that the words of Jesus be appended to the minority report: "You are the salt of the earth. But if the salt has lost its savor, wherewithal shall it be salted? It then serves no purpose but to be thrown out and be trampled on by men."

2. THE MAJORITY REPORT

The minority report won only sixteen votes. The majority of the delegates concluded that it was too concrete and that the evils mentioned, particularly institutional and structural evils, were too forthrightly named. The majority report was innocent of such specifics. But there is no reason at all for supposing that the majority report provides support for the apartheid laws. On the contrary. Anyone taking trouble to read it will see that the report condemns, be it with considerable caution, the principles and practices of apartheid just as severely as the minority report does. What the writers of the minority report feared, however, has happened. Delegates from South Africa gave interviews to the press and wrote articles in which they enthusiastically hailed the report for its refusal to make a judgment on apartheid. Their enthusiasm, however, can be supported only with falsehoods. The majority report will speak for itself to anyone who reads it for himself. And its importance must be underscored. Now an ecumenical organization of Calvinist churches around the world has said what already had been said at the Cottesloe conference and what is still being affirmed by almost every participant at that conference. Here we have a declaration not from a group of liberals or humanists or Communists, but from an international synod of conservative Reformed churches.

Three core recommendations can be used to summarize the majority as well as the minority report. The churches of South Africa are urged:

(1) To call for consultations with the leaders of all ethnic groups in order to consider steps that must be taken for the restructuring of society.

(2) To point the way for all groups to participate in political decision-making, and to stimulate processes to bring about such political co-responsibility.

(3) To demand that laws rooted in racial discrimination be abolished.

In my judgment all that was urged by the Cottesloe consultation, by the Uppsala Assembly, and by the "Message to the People of South Africa" is summed up in the recommendations made by the Reformed Ecumenical Synod. Herein the majority and minority reports are one; the only difference is that what was explicit in the minority report is implicit in the majority report.

D. The Message of the South African Council of Churches

We mentioned earlier the presence at the RES Assembly of the message that the South African Council of Churches had prepared for publication after the World Council had met in Uppsala. We will devote a few pages to this message because, in my opinion, it sets the conflict between the Christian Gospel and the ideology of apartheid in a new and decisive stage, a stage of history that will need the concern, the sympathy, the prayers, and the participation of all Christians. We have tried to show how the discriminatory laws and practices that are bound up with apartheid are rooted in a nationalistic ideology that falsely exploits the name of Christianity. For us it is an easy thing to make this judgment. But for those who wrote and published this message, the cost has been high in personal pain, conflict, and self-denial. Exposing the gap between Gospel and ideology is not a job for weak men in South Africa.

The Council of Churches was not intimidated by the possibilities of hostility, and in June of 1968 it addressed the people of South Africa with its powerful appeal. The message was drawn up by its theological commission, and the Council directed the same commission to have it published and distributed. It is addressed to every individual member of the churches and to the churches as a whole as a "basis for study and action." Further, individuals and churches were urged to sign the document as a public expression of their commitment. Meanwhile, *Kairos*, the bulletin published by the Council, regularly carries reactions to the message as they come in. From *Kairos* it is clear that the message has had a very hard time gaining acceptance among the churches: fear and doubts prevail, and many are reluctant to put their signatures on it. The President of the Republic has taken note of it, and reacted to it with threats: "Clerical garb," he warned, "is not going to protect these spiritual leaders" if they attempt to translate this message into deeds.

Here then is the message.

A MESSAGE TO THE PEOPLE OF SOUTH AFRICA

"In the name of Jesus Christ.

"We are under an obligation to confess anew our commitment to the universal faith of Christians, the eternal Gospel of salvation and security in Christ alone.

"1. *What the Christian Gospel says.* The Gospel of

Jesus Christ is the good news that in Christ God has broken down the walls of division between God and man, and therefore also between man and man.

"The Gospel of Jesus Christ declares that Christ is the truth who sets men free from all false hopes of grasping freedom for themselves, and that Christ liberates them from a pursuit of false securities.

"The Gospel of Jesus Christ declares that, in the crucifixion of Jesus, sin has been forgiven and God has met and mastered the forces that threaten to isolate man and destroy him.

"The Gospel of Jesus Christ declares that, in the resurrection of Jesus, God showed himself as the conqueror and destroyer of the most potent of all forms of separation, namely death, and he proved the power of his love to overthrow the evil powers of fear, envy, and pride, which cause hostility between men.

"The Gospel of Jesus Christ declares that, by this work of Christ, men are being reconciled to God and to each other, and that excluding barriers of ancestry, race, nationality, language, and culture have no rightful place in the inclusive brotherhood of Christian disciples. . . .

"2. *Our Concern.* This, in summary, is the Gospel of salvation in Jesus Christ. It offers hope and security for the whole life of man; it is to be understood not only in a mystical and ethical sense for the salvation of the individual person, and not only in a sacramental and ecclesiastical sense within the framework of the Church; the Gospel of Christ is to be understood in a cultural, social (and therefore political), cosmic and universal sense, as the salvation of the world and of human existence in its entirety.

"For this reason, Christians are called to witness to the significance of the Gospel in the particular circumstances of time and place in which they find themselves. We, in this country, and at this time, are in a situation where a policy of racial separation is being deliberately effected with increasing rigidity. The effects of this are to be seen in a widening range of aspects of life—in political, economic, social, educational, and religious life; indeed, there are few areas even of the private life of the individual which are untouched by the effects of the doctrine of racial separation. In consequence, this doctrine is being seen by many not merely as a temporary political policy but as a necessary and permanent expression of the will of God, and as the genuine form of Christian obedience for this country. But this doctrine, together with the hardships which are derivant from its implementations, forms a programme which is truly hostile to Christianity and can serve only to keep people away from the real knowledge of Christ.

"There are alarming signs that this doctrine of separation has become, for many, a false faith, a novel gospel which offers happiness and peace for the community and for the individual. It holds out to men a security built not on Christ but on the theory of separation and the preservation of their racial identity. It presents separate development of our race-groups as a way for the people of South Africa to save themselves. Such a claim inevitably conflicts with the Christian Gospel, which offers salvation, both social and individual, through faith in Christ alone.

"This false offer of salvation is being made in this country in the name of Christianity. Therefore, we believe that the Church must enable all our people to distinguish between this false, novel gospel and the true eternal Gospel of Jesus Christ. We believe that it is the Church's duty to enable our people to discriminate more carefully between what may be demanded of them as subjects or citizens of the State of South Africa and what is demanded of them as disciples of Jesus Christ.

"3. *The Gospel's Claim.* The Christian Gospel declares that there is no other name than that of Christ whereby men must be saved. Thus salvation in Christ exposes the falsity of hope of salvation through any other means. . . .

"But, in South Africa, everyone is expected to believe that a man's racial identity is the most important thing about him. Until a man's racial identity is established, virtually no decisions can be taken; but, once it is established, it can be stated where he can live, whom he can marry, what work he can do, what education he can get, whose hospitality he can accept, where he can get medical treatment, where he can be buried—and the answer to multitudes of other questions can be supplied once this vital fact is established. Thus, we are being taught that our racial identity is the final and all-important determining factor in the lives of men. As a result of this faith in racial identity, a tragic insecurity and helplessness afflicts those whose racial classification is in doubt. Without racial identity, it appears, we can do nothing: he who has racial identity has life; he who has not racial identity has not life. This amounts to a denial of the central statements of the Gospel. It is opposed to the Christian understanding of the nature of man and community. It, in practice, severely restricts the ability of Christian brothers to serve and know each other, and even to give each other simple hospitality. It arbitrarily limits the ability of a person to obey the Gospel's command to love his neighbor as himself.

"Any scheme which is claimed to be Christian must also take account of the reconciliation already made for us in Christ. The policy of separate development does not take proper account of these truths. It promises peace and harmony between the peoples of our country not by a faithful and obedient pursuit of the reconciliation wrought by Christ, but through separation, which, being precisely the opposite course, is a demonstration of unbelief and distrust in the power of the Gospel. Any demonstration of the reality of reconciliation would endanger this policy; therefore the advocates of this policy inevitably find themselves opposed to the Church if it seeks to live according to the Gospel and if it shows that God's grace has overcome our hostilities. A thorough policy of racial separation must ultimately require that the Church should cease to be the Church.

"Everywhere, sin corrupts God's creation; particularly,

it exploits differences to generate hostility. The policy of separate development is based on the domination of one group over all others; it depends on the maintenance of white supremacy; thus it is rooted in and dependent on a policy of sin. The Christian Gospel declares that God has acted to overthrow the policy of sin. God is bringing us from a living death to a new life; and one of the signs that this has happened is that we love the brethren. But, according to the Christian Gospel, our 'brethren' are not merely the members of our own race-group, nor are they the people with whom we may choose to associate. Our brother is the person whom God gives to us. To disassociate from our brother on the grounds of natural distinction is to despise God's gift and to reject Christ.

"The Gospel of Jesus Christ declares that God is love. This is not an easy doctrine. It is not 'sentimental humanism'. It is far easier to believe in a god who is less than love and who does not require a discipleship of love. But if God is love, separation is the ultimately opposite force to God. The will to be separate is the most complete refusal of the truth. Apartheid is a view of life and a view of man which insists that we find our identity in dissociation and in distinction from each other. A policy of separate development which is based on this concept therefore involves a rejection of the central beliefs of the Christian Gospel. It reinforces divisions which the Holy Spirit is calling the people of God to overcome. This policy is, therefore, a form of resistance to the Holy Spirit.

"Our task is to work for the expression of God's reconciliation here and now. We are not required to wait for a distant 'heaven' where all problems will have been solved. What Christ has done, he has done already. We can accept his work or reject it; we can hide from it or seek to live by it. But we cannot postpone it, for it is already achieved. And we cannot destroy it, for it is the work of the eternal God.

"Many of our people believe that their primary loyalty

must be to their group or tradition or political doctrine, and that this is how their faithfulness will be judged. But this is not how God judges us. In fact, this kind of belief is a direct threat to the true salvation of many people, for it comes as an attractive substitute for the claims of Jesus. It encourages a loyalty expressed in self-assertion: it offers a way of salvation with no cross. But God judges us, not by our faithfulness to a sectional group but by our willingness to be made new in the community of Christ. We believe that we are under an obligation to state that our country and Church are under God's judgment, and that Christ is inevitably a threat to much that is called 'the South African way of life'. We must ask ourselves what features of our social order will have to pass away if the lordship of Christ is to be fully acknowledged and if the peace of God is to be revealed as the destroyer of our fear.

"But we believe that Christ is Lord, and that South Africa is part of his world. We believe that his kingdom and its righteousness have power to cast out all that opposes his purposes and keeps men in darkness. We believe that the word of God is not bound, and that it will move with power in these days, whether men hear or whether they refuse to hear. And so we wish to put to every Christian person in this country the question which we ourselves are bound to face each day: to whom, or to what are you truly giving your first loyalty, your primary commitment? Is it to a subsection of mankind, an ethnic group, a human tradition, a political idea; or to Christ?

"May God enable us to be faithful to the Gospel of Jesus Christ, and to be committed to Christ alone!"

This message is a courageous exposé of the ideological roots of apartheid. Churches outside South Africa should make it known that they support it—"coram publico et Deo." When the Barmen Declaration was made in Germany during the period of Hitler, churches outside of Germany stood silent, and by their silence left the spokesmen for the Confessing Church of Germany in isolation. The World Council has already supported the South African message. But now those churches who are still in fellowship with the Reformed churches of South Africa should let their support be known.

E. The Declarations of the World Alliance of Reformed Churches in Kenya, 1970

With the theme "God Reconciles and God Liberates," the Alliance of Reformed Churches met in Nairobi, Kenya, in August of 1970. During the conference, the tensions between races in areas where member churches live came under discussion. South Africa came in for review, since the Dutch Reformed Church of South Africa has retained membership in the Alliance. One passage in the conference's concluding report applies to this church:

> The practice of racial segregation by the Dutch Reformed Churches of South Africa within its own life, and the impression it gives of supporting the government in its policy and practice of racial segregation and white supremacy, along with the inertia of other churches with respect to their calling to resist oppression and injustice, is a matter of particular concern for us.

The passage was adopted by a vote of 111 to 82. The South African delegates expressed fear that "the sharp formulation will have an unfavorable influence on relations in South Africa." But they did not oppose a motion to hold a consultation among churches in South Africa under the auspices of the Alliance, and this motion for a consultation passed overwhelmingly. Not surprisingly, this did not sit well at home. Dr. J. S. Gericke, moderator of the Dutch Reformed Church of South Africa, soon made known his opposition to any such consultation on the grounds that the Alliance is clearly in disagreement with the stand of the Dutch Reformed Church.

MOVEMENTS FOR CHANGE

South Africa is a land where blacks and whites and many other groups of people will have to learn to live together. This prospect creates such dread among many people that they see no future for themselves except by keeping a stubborn hold on white domination over all other groups of people. Others sincerely believe that white supremacy is part of a God-given mandate to build a multiracial society in justice and love. Both groups are closed to alternatives.

Jürgen Moltmann said once that history does not consist so much of facts as of chances. Chances can be turned down, or fouled up. They can also be seized in faith and love. Whether grabbing hold of opportunities results in success or failure is beside the point. What is to the point is whether we seize them in obedience. There are people in South Africa who do want to search for and seize opportunities for alternatives.

Among those who honestly looked for workable alternatives to apartheid I must mention the great son of the Xhosas, the late Prof. Z. K. Matthews, who with a priestly heart and a prophetic urgency labored until he died without succumbing to hatred. This book is dedicated to his memory.

There are many who today are involved in the quest for alternatives to the present situation. Among them are both individuals and organizations.

The Institute for Race Relations should be mentioned first. In 1922 Johannesburg experienced serious race disturbances, aggravated among other things by a miners' strike. During that period, it happened that Dr. Jesse Jones and Dr. William Aggrey were in South Africa. The tensions were so great that at the initiation of these two men a regional multiracial council was established and an interracial conference was held. Out of the conference came the decision in 1928 to set up the Institute, and it was launched the following year. This institute has done more than any other single group to give expert guidance, gather facts on the actual situation between the races, and promote peace, goodwill, and practical cooperation between the races. It publishes a yearbook along with occasional papers and pamphlets. Its director, F. Van Wyk, who has been associated with the Institute for several years, is a member of the Dutch Reformed Church. He believes that a basic change of attitude in the church is of uppermost importance for the future of the country.

The position of the Institute in South Africa has become very precarious. Its work is distrusted and harassed by the present regime. Yet it goes on and is of enormous value. Van Wyk said recently: "I was lately invited to become a Professor in Canada, and if organizations like this Institute . . . are finally kept from functioning, I shall have to leave the land of my birth. But I am going to stay for now, if only because these symbols of hope are still present."

I should again mention the South African Council of Churches. It can only be mourned that the Afrikaner churches (i.e., the three Reformed churches) have deserted the council. One of the things that Reformed churches elsewhere can do here is to try to restore communication between the English-speaking churches who are members of the council and the Afrikaans-speaking churches who are not.

A third agent of change is the Christian Institute of South Africa. This institute has a multiracial and ecumenical staff, under its two directors C. F. Beyers Naudé and J. de Bruin. Since its beginning in 1963, it has made extraordinary efforts to bring about a change of mind and structure in society at large, and to build bridges between the large groups of independent churches. A fourth agent of change is the study project called Sprocas, supported by the Christian Institute and the Council of Churches. The purpose of the project is to give the "Message to the People of South Africa" hands and feet by working out concrete alternative proposals for the reorganization of life in the whole of South African society.

The University Christian Movement must also be mentioned. It is led by an ex-priest, Colin B. Collins, who was secretary of the Catholic bishops for eleven years, and by a Methodist, Rev. Basil Moore. When the federation of Christian students was forced by apartheid policies to split up into separate racial groups, the UCM arose in its place in an effort to keep interracial and ecumenical student contacts alive. Thus, there now exist two student organizations, with precious little contact between them—the UCM, which keeps up relations with the World Federation of Christian Students, and the racially segregated Association of Christian Students, which is oriented toward the Inter-varsity Fellowship. The UCM has been accused of being theologically anemic, but whatever its theological shortcomings are, it can never be accused of sidestepping real problems. In spite of heavy opposition, including government hostility, in spite of the government's refusal to give Basil Moore a passport to leave the country, and in spite of the fact that the UCM is not permitted on several campuses, its members persist in their work. One of the most impressive pieces to come out of this group is a study of Black Theology, which has been a ferment among black African students to stimulate group consciousness among themselves. The UCM makes much of genuine personal relationships for the sake of Christ, and this is its basic reason for resisting segregation frontally.

Talking with a South African about these "groups for change," I was reminded of still another—though unorganized—group. These are the students, assistants, and professors in places like the Universities of Stellenbosch and Potchefstroom who are well aware that apartheid is wrong and unworkable, and who know that change has got to come. In contacts with young sociologists, anthropologists, and philosophers, I have often been impressed with the profound skepticism that prevails among them, along with a yearning for a change in the mentality and political direction of the country. Unfortunately, these feelings are expressed mostly in intimate private groups. There is little inclination for nonconformity and for individual public expression of convictions. But it will not always be so. The time is coming when the silence will be broken and the younger intellectuals in and out of the Reformed churches will come out in the open and work for that longed-for change of mind and course.

THE WAY OUT OF SOUTH AFRICA'S DILEMMA

What is the core of South Africa's dilemma? At the moment, South Africa is a country in which power is controlled by a monopoly of "white superiors." Undeniably, this group has managed to do some good for the other, subordinate groups. But everything that is done happens within the framework of this white power monopoly. This white monopoly cannot endure any more than it can be morally justified. A child can see that the struggle for "black power" is growing everywhere, even though its organized emergence is now put down within a hard hand. A polarization is taking place between the ruling white monopolists and those who seek an equally segregated black power monopoly. South Africa exists within the two poles of a present white monopoly and a potential black monopoly. It sometimes looks as though the tension is doomed to follow a fated course in the style of a Greek tragedy. But the sign of hope is the emergence of enlightened and courageous people among the Colored, the Bantu, and the Indian communities, as well as among the whites, who pin their hopes on a new distribution of power among all the peoples and on a society of cooperation in place of apartheid. The future of South Africa lies with those who strive for a modern, pluralist society, in which all groups participate in the decision-making of the whole community, and take their fair share in the exercise of power. The Sermon on the Mount speaks its woes to the rich and powerful who will not share, speaks its blessings to those "who hunger after righteousness," and summons all to share with those who have not. Sharing of political power, sharing of economic power, sharing of cultural power, sharing of social power—this is the only alternative to the present power monopoly of one group over another. The way of justice is not the way of forced, arbitrarily regulated segregation; it is the way of sharing power, the way of reasonable cooperation among all groups in a search for justice. South Africa is a country with extraordinary wealth and extraordinary poverty. It has a fairly limited population and an enormously expansive frontier, along with incredible economic potential. It is a land in which prosperity and justice for everyone can be gained and guaranteed if the white top-layer will only let itself be awakened to a new way of looking at life, and learns the secret of the word "share." James Baldwin was right when he said that the churches in South Africa hold the keys to a change of spirit and that a change could come over South Africa if the churches only had the will and courage to lead the way to it.

Chapter Six

Epilogue: Faith and Involvement

Before closing shop on this book, I want to emphasize
that the struggle for racial justice is not and never can be
a struggle going on out there apart from us; it is a struggle
that calls everyone of us to personal faith and involvement. Theological insight is no substitute for engagement.
Sociological analysis and scholarly judgments about
where the tender spots in race relations lie are not enough
to qualify us as contributors to the solutions. The struggle demands a personal stake.

Where can we find the impetus for faith? Where can we
get the spirit to make a commitment?

One day at the General Assembly of the World Council, W. A. Visser 't Hooft called together the delegates
who had been at the first world youth conference in
Amsterdam back in 1939. That conference had left behind some very deep and lasting impressions that had
filtered through to the reality level of some of our lives.
With memories reviewed by our reunion in Uppsala, I
recalled the conference vividly, and I would like to end
this book by passing on a few of those vivid recollections.

The clouds of World War II hung heavy over that
crowd of Christian young people. Young men and women
of all races were there, and the conflicts already begun
and the conflicts that lay ahead preoccupied us all. We
sensed something of our collective guilt, of the fault that
lay in the lives of all our countries and races. We were

aware of the accusations that our countries were hurling back and forth at each other, of the hate and the pride that had infected the relations between people of the races that we all represented. These things were talked about openly, with a candor possible only when everyone meeting is aware of being in the presence of a living God.

At the end, we took communion together in one of the local churches. Jesus Christ was the host. We felt, as we took bread and wine together, something of how we had hurt Him, and killed Him, and how we do it every day in our own time. We felt as though we had to take the blame that people everywhere were throwing at each other and bring it here against ourselves.

All at once, ignoring the planned liturgy, a Chinese student, whose country had already been invaded by Japan, stood up in his pew. I can still recall his words accurately, as he translated our feelings for us. He said: "I drink from this cup because I believe that the blood of Jesus Christ, the Son of God and the Son of man, was spilled as an atonement for my sins and the sins of my people. For He who died for us is risen from the dead." Then he looked to a Japanese student sitting across from him and said to him: "I would hate you with all my heart if I did not know that Jesus died for your sins and the sins of your people." With this, he reached his cup out and handed it to the Japanese student, and said: "Take this, drink it, remember and believe that the blood of Jesus Christ was shed for a complete remission of all our sins."

I realized at that moment, for the first time really, that the reconciliation and pardon given us in Jesus Christ applies not only to our private sins, but to our collective sins and to the sinful structures that shape injustice between nations and races. There, for the first time, I realized that what Jesus Christ did for us has cosmic dimensions, that it touches the whole ecumenical family of nations.

Working as a chaplain among Asian students before the

war, I began to feel the hurt, the suffering, the guilt that our colonial practices had injected into race relations. After 1939 came the years of war in Indonesia, and with them my years of imprisonment; after that came the hostilities between the Netherlands and Indonesia. During all those rough years, the secret of what had happened at the Lord's table in Amsterdam took on even deeper meaning.

I shall also never forget the first communion service I attended after the war, a Dutchman in a Javanese congregation in Jakarta during a time of revolution. Nor shall I ever forget the first general session of the World Council in 1948; on my left hand sat Martin Niemoller and on my right the Japanese delegate, Dr. Ebisawa. The power of reconciliation was alive between us. Then there was the conference of Afro-Asian countries in Bandung in 1955, where one evening Richard Wright sat with an American friend and me and told us his life story. Years later, I came to know Z. K. Matthews, who has become my dear Bantu friend. In this way, slowly, on an experiential level, the scope of my consciousness grew into a broad awareness that the racial question had global dimensions that can only grow larger. And it also dug deeper into my consciousness that the indispensable condition for a healing of these relations is the forgiveness of sins: reconciliation is the door to restored justice, the motive for digging in and keeping at the struggle for righteousness through every setback.

I am absolutely convinced that the source for strength to continue the struggle lies with forgiveness and reconciliation through Christ. The question that haunts me is whether we in the West, who like to think of ourselves as the inheritors of "Western civilization," do in fact live out of this faith and power? Or is faith and its power dead and buried? James Baldwin put the question to us that notable evening at Uppsala when the race question came up: "I ask myself whether there is still the moral power, the spiritual courage still left within our 'Christian culture' to show repentance and to be born again and to do the works of freedom." This is surely *the* question.

My own life's history has convinced me that contact with Christians in Asia, Africa, and Latin America can be used by God to bring power back into the lives of Western Christians. At the Notting Hill consultation, Robert Nelson told of a fresco done by Giotto in the Basilica of St. Francis that captures the moment of Lazarus' awakening from death. Jesus had spoken the life-bringing word. Around Him stand several white people. But the man who puts out his hand to help Lazarus out of the tomb is black. Could it be that we Western white people need to take the hand of fellow Christians from Africa, or Asia, or Latin America to be helped out of our dead faith into a new power of life? Churches are dying in many parts of the Western world, and a faith with power for reconciliation and forgiveness is hard to find. Perhaps contact with African, Asian, or Latin Christians can set us on the way again to fight for racial justice in the strength of shared faith.

Resistance to the struggle is incredibly strong. Efforts to break through the status quo, truly to break down the walls of division, run hard against enormous commercial, political, social, and psychological obstacles. But what does the Lord want of us if it is not to seek justice? What could Jesus Christ demand of us, He who tore down the walls that separate the races, if it is not to cross over the rubble and together tear down those walls we have built again.

We may do well to remember an episode from Jesus' life whenever we meet resistance. One time, Jesus' mother and brothers decided that Jesus had probably gone too far, that prudence demanded He retreat and call it off. Here was the voice of blood relations, the voice of one's own group, the voice of self-interest, the voice of clan and family, all saying: "Give up the fight." But Jesus said, "Anyone who does the will of God is my brother and sister and mother" (Mark 3:35).

It is the Father's will that justice prevail between the races and that all the walls separating them be broken down. What does it matter if eyebrows are raised and if vested interests are threatened by the struggle? He who does the will of the Father in the struggle for racial justice belongs among those walking together towards God's ecumenopolis, the New Jerusalem, the new earth, "where justice dwells."

Rhodesia

The consultation on racism that met in Notting Hill in May of 1969 gave considerable attention to the troubled country of Rhodesia. The moral wounds that need healing today lie particularly open and bloody for the world and church to see in Rhodesia. Here the relationships between the rich and the poor are not carried on at a distance, as is often the case elsewhere. Here the relationships between the rich white community and the poor township, or reservation, are carried on in everyone's immediate presence. The rich and the poor are not removed by thousands of miles. To make this plain, we should take a quick, bird's-eye view of this territory.

The Federation of Rhodesia and Nyasaland was created in 1953, made up of three separate British territories, Southern Rhodesia, Nyasaland, and Northern Rhodesia. Each of these was the product of the crudest acts of colonization in British experience, dating back to the taking of Mashonaland in 1890. The Governor of the new Federation was Sir Roy Welensky. Welensky's ambition was limited independence for Rhodesia, under white control. The man who saw through and fought this raw attempt to give undivided power to a white minority was the former missionary Reginald Stephen Garfield Todd, Prime Minister of Southern Rhodesia from 1953 to 1958. He spoke for the black population, who trusted him, and he sought a multiracial society with equal rights for all, the abandonment of all discriminatory laws, and the release of all political prisoners—that is, all who were put in prison for their roles in the fight for equal rights. Todd realized that Welensky's dream ought not and was not going to come true, that no small white minority could permanently exercise complete control over a large black majority.

The Federation soon began to fall apart. Nyasaland became independent and took the name Malawi. Northern Rhodesia became Zambia. But in Southern Rhodesia a movement was undertaken by Ian Douglas Smith and his Front Party to keep white rule in a land where blacks outnumbered whites by five million to one-quarter of a million people. The purpose of the Front has always been to maintain the power monopoly enjoyed by the whites. Even before the Republic was proclaimed, a series of discriminatory laws were passed that showed all the earmarks of influence from South Africa. Meanwhile, Smith and his colleagues wrote up a constitution for a wholly independent Rhodesia with a wholly white minority as its political power base. Formally, provision is made for the representation in parliament of every racial group; but the representation of each racial group is based on the relative financial contribution each group makes via the income tax. Now while the blacks, because of their overwhelming majority, deliver a far greater amount by way of *indirect* taxes, they pay only 5 percent of the income tax, the small amount being a direct consequence of white economic imperialism. And obviously, given the economic classification in Rhodesia, it will take an eternity before the blacks will be in a position to pay as much income tax as do the whites, and thus to gain 50 percent of the seats in parliament. But this is the way the constitution stipulates it. The English government has taken the view that she is not permitted to give Rhodesia its independence until it offers effective guarantees that it is working towards a majority rule. Smith's constitution effectively rules out majority rule for any imaginable future.

On November 28, 1965, the Roman Catholic bishops published a statement of protest against the Smith regime's minority rule in the face of an overwhelming majority who have no role in it. But Smith and his colleagues have driven on, ignoring the judgment of the British government, the United Nations, and most of the world's churches. The Republic became a fact. The independence of Rhodesia was declared in November of 1965. The following June, the few who had voting rights in Rhodesia had to make a choice for or against the apartheid constitution. Needless to say, the majority of this tiny minority opted for a constitution which excluded the vast majority of the people from even deciding whether they wished to be ruled by it, a constitution which in fact introduced a parliamentary dictatorship. The minority chose a constitution that would legalize the oppression of black Africans within their own land.

The Council of Churches in Rhodesia along with the Roman Catholic Church immediately spoke against the constitution. Practically all the churches, with the exception of the Dutch Reformed Church, called for multiracial goverment, declaring that an all-white government is as morally objectionable to the churches as an all-black government would be. Only a multiracial government that provided equal rights to all could be acceptable to the churches.

Acceptance of the constitution was just the first step. In the spring of 1970, the second was taken. The independent republic broke its ties with the English crown and the Union Jack was hauled down. Consolidation of a white racist state in Rhodesia was now in its second stage. Five million blacks are represented in parliament by sixteen men. Of these sixteen, the majority are conservative tribal chiefs who are in fact servants of the government. Backed by this sort of parliament, Ian Smith is pushing apartheid through on every level of life. One of the crudest forms is the Land Tenure Act, which regulates the division of available lands.

This act, modeled after South Africa's apartheid laws

and enacted by the white minority, means that the whites, 5 percent of the population, own an amount of land equal to that allotted to the remaining 95 percent. Moreover, the white half is made up of the most fertile lands and the most valuable parts of the cities. Blacks may work in the white territories, but only as migrant laborers with all the attendant miseries that accompany the migratory system.

PROTEST FROM THE CHURCHES

The churches of Rhodesia have protested in many ways against this and similar laws. The Roman Catholic Church has taken the lead here, declaring that if they are forced to comply with the apartheid policy of racial segregation, they will close down their schools, orphanages, homes for the aged, and the like. The Protestant Council of Churches also plays its role in resistance (the exception here is the Dutch Reformed Church, which is associated with the Dutch Reformed Church of South Africa). Several other churches have threatened to close their schools if the Smith regime forces them to apply its racial laws. In fact, the Ecumenical Press Service has pointed out that the only organized power bloc resisting the present regime is the churches. The Secretary of Internal Affairs has publicly accused the churches of sabotage and sedition, remarking that Satan's fork is disguised as a bishop's staff. The churches, however, insist that theirs is not a political resistance, but a spiritual one, because the new laws are forcing people to disobey God's demands and frustrate His promises.

When Kenneth Shelton, the former bishop of Matabeleland, one of the original two components of Southern Rhodesia, was forced to resign as the chairman of the Council of Churches of Rhodesia, he made this remark:

> The future of Christianity in this land depends on whether it is prepared, really prepared to break down the walls that divide mankind. If it fails here, it will rightly be rejected.

But if it does fail, no one will be able to say that the Gospel has lost its power, only that men lost their courage to preach and live it concretely. The Gospel is not preached merely through declarations made by conferences, it is preached by the convictions of those who will no longer tolerate the existence of the walls of division.

The Rhodesian issue is, like the South African issue, a global concern. We all have a share in it. The question of what God wants done hovers over the oppressors and the oppressed; it presses in on the British and the United Nations; it bears on the guerilla fighters being trained even now by Joshua Nkomo, and it is set before the churches of Jesus Christ.

Appendix Two

Interracial Marriage

I have had occasion to mention South Africa's Immorality Act, which not only brands interracial marriage as a moral vice, but threatens it with punishment. Since racial mixing is a sensitive matter in many parts of the world, we should devote some attention to it as an ethical issue. This would be pointless if interracial marriage were not so often looked on as something immoral. But unfortunately it is. We have in our time seen the Nazi idiocy of "pure blood" propagated with the moral fervency of a religion. In South Africa, as we have seen, the prohibition of interracial marriage is buttressed with pseudo-theological authority. And in the United States, the overtones of moral feelings against it prevail even where the letter of old laws against it may be dead. So it will serve our purpose to take a hard look at the ethical issues that are involved.

We should note first that racial mixing is as old as mankind. Wherever the opportunity has presented itself, wherever people of difference races have met each other, they have tended to marry. All the great regional cultures have arisen out of a mixing of races. But those great cultures that were born of racial mixing then isolated themselves from one another, and so we find the Western, the Chinese, the Indian, and the African cultures. During the last five hundred years, however, these various communities and cultures have again met each other and the mixture has begun again. Racial mixing went on for some four hundred years under the shadow of slavery, colonial take-overs, and imperialist domination. But now we are entering a period in which racial contacts, in a world becoming one, will take on a more voluntary style and will probably increase and occur on a much freer basis.

All over the world, large numbers of people live and work together who are products of racial mixing. The largest number live in North and South America, products of a mixture of blacks and whites, and Indians and whites. Paraguay's population is 97 percent of mixed blood. More than 70 percent of Venezuela's population is born of interracial background. Peru, Bolivia, and Ecuador have percentages similar to these. Taken as a whole, people of mixed blood form about one-sixth of the population of North and South America. The people of Hawaii are almost wholly a mixture. In Asia the number of people who have come from a mixture of Chinese and Polynesian people and of whites and Polynesians is very large. In Africa too, especially South Africa, a large percentage of the people have grown from mixed marriages.

But my intention here is not to provide statistics on mixed races. I only wish to recall that racial intermarriage is a very old thing, that in some areas racial mixing has occurred on a large scale indeed, and that this mixing is likely to go on increasingly in the future. Racial mixing is simply a fact that we must deal with. That in the first place.

Secondly, there is no biological reason to oppose racial mixture. And yet there is no issue about which more ignorance and prejudice is ventilated: "Mixing leads to physical deterioration"; or "inferior qualities of both races tend to dominate"; and so forth. Nonsense like this is not only heard over coffee cups, but is passed on in pseudo-scientific publications as well. UNESCO has done the service of setting most of these misapprehensions to rest through a series of studies on the race problem. Harry L.

Shapiro has included in this series a book on *Race Mixture* that answers the prejudices with biological data drawn from specific instances. No proof has ever been given that racial mixing leads to an inferior race. On the contrary, it is sometimes beneficial: from a biological point of view, some racial mixing is more defensible than is racial exclusivism.

Finally, there are the social and psychological aspects of racial mixing. One commonplace has it that racial mixing stretches its evil consequences to the offspring socially and psychologically for many generations, but this is altogether too general. The social and psychic aftereffects of racial mixing depend almost wholly on how a society judges racial mixing in the first place. A society that is accustomed to and accepts racial mixing renders no social or psychic harm to children of racially mixed marraiges. All one need do is think of Brazil, Peru, Hawaii, Jamaica, and many other places, where the offspring of racial mixing are not in the slightest harmed by social judgment (though there may well be other kinds of social and psychological pressures). But where a society is hostile and judgmental toward racial mixing, you have a situation where the offspring will be disadvantaged socially and psychologically. There the parents as well as the children are condemned to live under the curse of this prejudice "to the third and fourth generation."

It can happen that a community consisting of racially mixed people is isolated and forms a distinct caste that is manipulated and forced into a servile role in the social stratification. These people may be generally put down as products of vice and loose morals, as happens in South Africa. But this sort of social-psychological effect of racial mixing must not be generalized. And it must be remembered that these problems are caused not by the mixing, but by the brutal devices of pride, hypocrisy, contempt, and the like. The children are then caught between racial arrogance and stupidity on the one hand and the struggle for power among the races on the other.

An analysis of the social and psychological effects of racial mixing does not lead us to conclude that bad effects are caused by racial mixing as such—but it does convince us that the sinful structures that bring about the bad effects must be contested and changed.

So we now face the question of the morality of racial mixing as such: Are there theologically grounded moral objections to racial mixing? The answer must be loud and clear: *There is not a single moral objection to interracial marriage.* We are not now talking about the ethics of marriage in general, nor about God's promises and commands that qualify every decision to marry. The only question that concerns us is whether God prohibits interracial marriage. And the answer to that question is unequivocally *No.*

To turn to the Bible, the Old Testament tells us of many interracial marriages without a hint of judgment or criticism of them. Joseph, the favorite son of Jacob and the protector of the sons of Israel, married the daughter of an Egyptian priest of Heliopolis. Moses, who led the people of Israel out of Egypt and who mediated God's Law, married a daughter of a Midianite priest, Jethro. Esther married a Persian prince. In the genealogy of Jesus are four women who are non-Israelites. The rules found in Ezra and Nehemiah forbidding mixed marriages after the exile have nothing at all to do with racial mixing; they were meant to protect Israel temporarily from involvement with other people for the sake of the *religious* function Israel was called to serve among the Gentiles.

The New Testament breaks down even that wall of separation. The Christian communities of the New Testament embraced interracial marriage commonly. Timothy, the son of a Jewish mother and a Greek father, was completely accepted as a kind of connecting link by both the Jewish and the Gentile Christians, a prototype of those people who were born of interracial marriages and who found their identity in Jesus Christ, the source of their trust and their love.

I do not mean to belittle the problems that some
societies create for interracial marriages, problems for the
marriage partners and for their children. I only mean to
deny that the interracial dimension of the marriages conflicts with God's will. In fact, those who contend that
interracial marriages violate God's will are themselves
misusing the name of the Lord. The Immorality Act that
is the law in South Africa is an immoral law.

I will end this section with some relevant words of
J. H. Oldham on the subject:

> Racial difference in itself forms no insurmountable hin-
> drance to the most intimate human relations. A marriage
> between persons of differing races, but with compatible
> character and temperament, can be happier than persons of
> the same race whose temperaments and character are not
> compatible. Freedom and creativity are of great social val-
> ue, and venturesomeness and willingness to *try* can be as
> useful in this arena as in others. Inter-racial marriages can
> contribute something to a deeper reciprocal understanding
> between different races, an understanding of a sort that will
> be of indispensable value if the people of the world are one
> day going to live together in a spirit of unity.